Galatians
Ephesians

Armin J. Panning

SAINT LOUIS

The interior illustrations were originally executed by James Tissot (1836–1902).

Commentary and pictures are reprinted from Galatians, Ephesians (The People's Bible Series), copyright © 1997 by Northwestern Publishing House. Used by permission.

Copyright © 1997 Concordia Publishing House
3558 S. Jefferson Avenue, St. Louis, MO 63118-3968
Manufactured in the United States of America

1 2 3 4 5 6 7 8 9 10   06 05 04 03 02 01 00 99 98 97

CONTENTS

MAPS

ILLUSTRATIONS

PREFACE

The People's Bible Commentary is just what the name implies—a Bible and commentary for the people. It includes the complete text of the Holy Scriptures in the popular New International Version. The commentary following the Scripture sections contains personal applications as well as historical background and explanations of the text.

The authors of *The People's Bible Commentary* are men of scholarship and practical insight, gained from years of experience in the teaching and preaching ministries. They have tried to avoid the technical jargon which limits so many commentary series to professional Bible scholars.

The most important feature of these books is that they are Christ-centered. Speaking of the Old Testament Scriptures, Jesus himself declared, "These are the Scriptures that testify about me" (John 5:39). Each volume of *The People's Bible Commentary* directs our attention to Jesus Christ. He is the center of the entire Bible. He is our only Savior.

We dedicate these volumes to the glory of God and to the good of his people.

The Publishers

GALATIANS
INTRODUCTION TO GALATIANS

Recipients

The opening paragraph of this little letter informs us that it is being sent "to the churches in Galatia." That sounds simple enough, but just where were those churches located? Actually, a surprising amount of discussion has centered on that question.

Fortunately, a definite answer to that question is not absolutely essential for understanding the letter. The Holy Spirit has here given us a letter that stands by itself and remains useful for all ages and situations, for it answers the most basic of all questions: How can the sinner be put right with God?

While identifying the recipients of this letter is not absolutely essential, the assumptions we make about where the Galatians lived will influence our interpretation at various points. It is necessary, therefore, briefly to address this matter.

Regarding the general locale of Galatia, there is no doubt. Galatia was located in the central part of Asia Minor, that is, in the heart of modern Turkey. Differences of opinion arise when one tries to become more specific than that. The Galatian people, immigrants from Gaul (ancient France), lived in the northern part of central Turkey. "Galatia" could refer to the territory where these "Galatian" people lived. Or it could refer to the province the Romans named Galatia, a considerably larger area that extended much farther south. Because of the difference between these geographical areas, Paul could hardly have had both in mind.

The view of this writer is that Paul was addressing congregations in the southern area, in the Roman province. To be

Important places in Paul's letter to the Galatians

specific, these would be the congregations in and around Antioch, Iconium, Lystra, and Derbe. This is precisely the area of activity described in some detail by Luke in Acts 13 and 14, where he tells us of Paul's first missionary journey.

Date

Interestingly enough, *where* the recipients of Paul's letter lived has a direct bearing on *when* he would have written to them.

If the letter was written to congregations in northern Galatia, we would have to use a later date. From what we can learn in Acts, Paul did not travel to any northern areas of Asia Minor until his second and third missionary journeys, and pertinent passages (16:6; 18:23) talk only of Paul passing through the area, with no reference to his founding congregations there. But assuming for the moment that he did establish congregations there, any letter to them would have to have been written later than the second or third missionary journey. Add to this the fact that some of Paul's statements in the letter to the Galatians (for example, 4:13) make it fair to assume that he had visited Galatia at least twice before writing his letter.

Our view that Paul was writing to cities in southern Galatia implies an earlier date and results in the following scenario. Paul had visited the cities in southern Galatia on his first missionary journey (about A.D. 50). Then, on his second missionary journey (A.D. 51–53), after the Council of Jerusalem described in Acts 15, he again traversed this southern territory, distributing the decisions of the council (Acts 16:4).

From this Galatian territory Paul then continued on his second missionary journey, which took him to Macedonia and Greece. It would seem that not too long after his departure from Galatia trouble arose in those congregations, for

Paul is "astonished" that they are "so quickly deserting" their former position (1:6). All this argues for the assumption that the book of Galatians may well have been written during the latter half of Paul's second missionary journey.

The time can perhaps be pinpointed even a bit closer. From the fact that the letter contains no greeting from Timothy or Silas, key figures in the work among the Galatians and hence well-known to those congregations, the letter may date to that period of Paul's work in Corinth before these coworkers had rejoined him (Acts 18:1-5). If the letter can be traced to the time of Paul's work in Corinth, that would date it about the year A.D. 52 and make Galatians the first epistle Paul wrote.

Occasion for writing

We have assumed that soon after Paul left Galatia a problem developed there that required his immediate attention. Apparently distance and the press of other duties (for example, starting a new mission in Corinth) prevented Paul from going to Galatia to attend to the matter in person. Hence he wrote them a letter, our epistle to the Galatians.

The content of that letter and particularly the tone in which it was written give us an indication of the urgency of the situation. Paul viewed the problem as nothing less than a frontal attack on the Galatians' faith and life. A substitute gospel— actually "no gospel at all" (1:7)—was being urged on his Galatians. If they accepted it, they would shipwreck their faith. It was a life-and-death matter that required an urgent and immediate letter.

But what was the source and nature of this attack on Paul's beloved Galatians? Actually, the attack came from a rather familiar source: Jewish opposition.

Recall Paul's pattern of doing mission work as it is described for us in Acts. Paul regularly aimed his efforts toward urban population centers. (This, incidentally, is another argument favoring a southern location for the Galatians. There were virtually no cities in the north.) In the populous urban areas Paul sought out Jewish synagogues where the Old Testament Law and the Prophets were regularly read and studied.

Paul's message to these synagogue worshipers was very basic. He told them: "The Savior promised in the whole Old Testament has come. It's Jesus of Nazareth. He lived a perfect life and died an innocent death on the cross for the sins of all people."

It was a disarmingly simple plan of salvation that Paul presented. He urged them: "Repent of your sins. Turn in faith to this Jesus of Nazareth. Accept his forgiveness and you can be sure that you are God's children and heirs of eternal salvation."

The initial reaction in the synagogues was joyful acceptance of so gracious a message. But invariably some had second thoughts. They began to wonder: "With salvation as a free gift, what happens to the regulations Moses gave us in the Old Testament? What about kosher foods, keeping a quiet Sabbath, circumcising sons on the eighth day? Are all these things suddenly of no value?"

It was a perceptive question they asked—and one that required a straightforward answer from Paul. He had to tell them that, as far as salvation was concerned, none of the ceremonies and Mosaic practices could bring them closer to God. If they wanted to observe their ancestral customs, they might do so *by choice*, but these customs were not to be required for salvation. Salvation was purely a gift from God.

That, of course, sounded like heresy to many with a synagogue-trained ear, and they reacted violently to Paul's teach-

5

ing of salvation purely by grace. Invariably, Paul was driven from the synagogue by such conservative Jewish opposition.

But Paul's exit from the synagogue did not mean the end of the Christian message. A minority of the synagogue worshipers accepted the message of salvation by grace alone and opened their homes as centers for the teaching of this liberating and life-giving gospel. When Paul moved on to other cities, these believers from the synagogue, who were thoroughly trained in God's Word, became the leaders of the fledgling "house churches" that soon grew into thriving Christian congregations. Growth in numbers came largely from Gentile converts who joined these congregations. The teaching and leadership positions, however, continued to be filled by the capable Jewish nucleus that had originally come from the synagogue.

In all this we see a reminder of what Jesus told the Samaritan woman at Jacob's well: "Salvation is from the Jews" (John 4:22). To a predominantly Gentile Galatia, Paul, a Jew, had proclaimed the message of a Jewish Jesus, and this message continued to be taught under the leadership of Jewish converts from the local synagogues. The Christian message brought to the Galatians was truly "from the Jews."

Recognizing that the Galatians depended so heavily upon Jewish leadership will go a long way toward understanding how the Galatians could be confused. Other Jewish teachers (perhaps from so prestigious a place as Jerusalem) had come to Galatia and challenged the local leaders regarding salvation purely by grace without keeping any of the Jewish customs and ceremonies.

Add to this the fact that these newly arrived teachers claimed to be Christian themselves. They did not deny the perfect life of Christ or his innocent death on the cross. Rather, they asserted that the way to receive the benefits of this Christ was through the time-honored method of joining God's covenant people, that is, by becoming "proselytes," converts to Judaism. Thus they urged the Galatians to believe in Christ *and* keep the Old Testament ceremonies.

That people would teach such a hybrid religion is not a product of our imagination. Scripture clearly describes such teachers. For example, these teachers made trouble for the Christians in Antioch of Syria by insisting that "unless you are circumcised, according to the custom taught by Moses, you cannot be saved" (Acts 15:1). And when a council was called in Jerusalem to settle this matter, they again showed their true colors. Luke tells us, "Then some of the believers who belonged to the party of the Pharisees stood up and said, 'The Gentiles must be circumcised and required to obey the law of Moses'" (verse 5).

Note that the troublemakers in Jerusalem are called "believers" in the sense that they wanted to align themselves with the Christians and claimed to believe in Christ. But they said some very unchristian things when they insisted that if people were to be saved, they had to be circumcised and obey the Law of Moses. That was a total denial of salvation by grace and really made Christ's work of no effect.

Teachers advocating acceptance of Christ on Jewish conditions are often referred to as "Judaizers." Examining Paul's letter to the Galatians leaves little doubt that such Judaizers had broken into the Galatian congregations and thoroughly upset the simple Christian faith of the Gentile believers. This, then, was the occasion of Paul's letter to the Galatians.

Content

Flaunting their supposed greater insight, these newly arrived Jewish teachers confronted the Gentile believers with a host of persuasive arguments. If we look at Paul's rebuttal, three main erroneous arguments seemed to be at the heart of the Judaizers' teaching:

- *You can't trust Paul's "gospel."* This is their logic: "How do you know that what Paul says about salvation by faith without any works is true when he himself is a 'nobody'? He wasn't a disciple or one of the Twelve whom Christ sent out. If the man is unknown, how can you trust his message?"
- *The Law of Moses is God's time-tested plan.* In contrast to Paul's "innovations," the Judaizers pointed to antiquity: "Look how long the Mosaic Law has been around! That is God's plan, his 'constitution,' on which he set up a people who have been uniquely his since the giving of the law at Mount Sinai. Isn't it much safer to join that nation by accepting its constitution and laws and thus make yourselves members of God's people and heirs of his salvation?"
- *Sinners need the law!* The Judaizers based their third argument on human nature: "People need guidance and direction. They will never respect God or treat their neighbor decently unless they have some pattern or standard to follow. And that pattern is there for you, tailor-made in the Mosaic Law."

Paul's letter to the Galatians addresses itself with remarkable vigor directly to those three points. It's a short letter, but powerful beyond its size. Its six chapters divide into a simple, three-part outline of two chapters each. In the first two chapters Paul takes up the matter of his being a "nobody" whose message must necessarily be unreliable.

In the third and fourth chapters he explains the true nature and character of the Mosaic Law in which the Judaizers were putting so much trust. In the last two chapters he shows that this law is not the real source and motivation for proper life and conduct.

As a preview of the specific arguments Paul will be using, let's elaborate on his three main points.

Chapters 1 and 2: Paul indicates the source of his gospel message, hence its reliability. Paul grants that he is not one of the Twelve, but that does not make his message unreliable. His message comes as much from Christ as that of the Twelve, for Paul was granted the unique experience of being confronted personally on the road to Damascus by the risen and ascended Christ. Christ called and commissioned him. Accordingly, Paul's message did not come from any human source or authority. It came from Christ himself.

Even though his message was not learned or derived from the Twelve, it was recognized and accepted by the Twelve. At the Council of Jerusalem they not only agreed with Paul's message, but they trusted him so much that they agreed to divide the mission field with him. The Twelve would continue to go to the Jews; Paul was to preach to the Gentiles. But the same gospel message would be preached to all, namely, salvation by faith in Christ without the requirement of keeping the Mosaic Law and ceremonies.

Chapters 3 and 4: Paul explains the timeless nature of the gospel, hence its superiority over the Mosaic Law, which came later and was only temporary.

After asking the Gentiles to recall how they first obtained their hope of salvation, Paul turns to the more objective example of Abraham. How was he saved? Why, he "believed God, and it was credited to him as righteousness" (3:6). He was saved *by faith*—and that before the Mosaic Law was ever given on Mount Sinai. Hence the Mosaic Law is obviously *not* the essence of God's plan of salvation.

The law was added a full four hundred years after the gospel promise had been given to Abraham. And even then the Mosaic Law was only temporary. It was limited to the Jewish nation and, even in their case, it was applicable only until the coming of Christ. Hence no one should now be required to keep the law for salvation. The believer in Christ is saved by faith alone without the observance of any law or ceremony. Such a person is free indeed.

Chapters 5 and 6: The gospel works true love for God and moves believers to do good works; hence the law is not necessary for motivating proper conduct in believers.

Faith in Christ not only frees believers *from* something (the demands of the law). It also frees them *for* something (a life of cheerful service to God and neighbor).

It is this freedom Paul extols in the closing chapters of his letter. He sets the tone for this entire section in the opening verse of the fifth chapter, where he declares, "It is for freedom that Christ has set us free." And he adds at once the admonition that dominates the letter: "Stand firm, then, and do not let yourselves be burdened again by a yoke of slavery."

To those who misconstrue liberty from the law as a license to do whatever they please Paul says, "Live by the Spirit, and you will not gratify the desires of the sinful nature" (5:16). Faith working by love will not result in unrestrained license. Rather, the fruit of the Spirit—love, joy, peace, and so on—will abound and flourish in a way the law could never produce. What folly, therefore, to return once more to subjection under the law and thus accept as master the "weak and miserable principles" (4:9) incapable of producing any good or blessing!

Continuing significance of the letter

In our day we are not plagued by Judaizers urging us to be good Christians by keeping the Law of Moses and by observing Old Testament ceremonies such as circumcision and kosher diets. And yet the same sort of pressure is brought to bear on all of us. Instinctively we feel an urgency to do something to get right with God. Burdened with a load of sin and guilt, we're susceptible to the thought "I'll have to do something to make things right with God." That makes sense to us.

In fact, the thought makes so much sense that at times it has been able to dominate and becloud the message of the Christian church. In medieval times the church began to proclaim a plan of salvation that in reality depended on human merit. Penance, good works, and merit earned by sacrificing the mass were coupled with the merit of Christ in such a way that heaven ultimately became a reward for properly observing church patterns and rituals.

It is not just a coincidence that Luther considered Galatians his favorite epistle. He was so attached to it that he could declare himself "betrothed" to this little epistle, that it was, in fact, his "Katherine von Bora."

Luther felt, and rightly so, that he was fighting the same battle with Rome that Paul had waged with the Judaizers. In both cases the answer to the false teachers had to be exactly the same: Salvation is not the result of Christ's merit and human effort working in combination. Salvation is purely the gift of God, by grace alone, through faith alone in Jesus Christ, without any works on man's part.

Heirs of the Reformation are not immune to the seductive thought that they should give some place to merit. Time and again the thought comes to us: "To be saved I'll have to become a better person. I dare not be as bad as others." That is assigning human merit an improper place in our thinking.

To fight against such thoughts we need again and again to return to Scripture's truth that the just shall live *by faith*. Nowhere is that truth set forth more clearly than in Paul's epistle to the Galatians. We too would do well to "betroth" ourselves to this little letter.

Outline of Galatians

Greeting 1:1-5

Introduction to the letter 1:6-10

I. Paul defends his apostleship 1:11–2:21
   A. Paul was called directly by Christ 1:11-24
      1. Paul's life before his conversion 1:11-14
      2. Circumstances surrounding Paul's conversion 1:15-17
      3. Paul's visit to Jerusalem three years after conversion 1:18-20
      4. Paul's stay in Syria and Cilicia 1:21-24
   B. Paul was received by the other apostles 2:1-21
      1. Paul's gospel was recognized at the Jerusalem Council 2:1-5
      2. An area of gospel work was accorded to Paul 2:6-10
      3. Peter accepts Paul's admonition 2:11-21

II. Paul explains justification—how the sinner becomes accepted before God 3:1–4:31
   A. Not by works, but by faith alone 3:1-18
      1. The Galatians' own experience 3:1-5
      2. Abraham's case 3:6-9
      3. The difference between law and gospel 3:10-14
      4. The promise given already to Abraham 3:15-18

B. Christians are free from the law 3:19-4:31
  1. A description of the law 3:19-29
  2. The parable of a minor heir, an illustration from everyday life 4:1-11
  3. Free from the law: the example of the Galatians' own conversion 4:12-20
  4. The example of Ishmael and Isaac (an allegory) 4:21-31

III. Paul explains sanctification—how the justified sinner is to live before God 5:1–6:10
  A. Encouragements that flow from the doctrine of justification 5:1–6:5
    1. Stand firm in your Christian liberty 5:1-12
    2. Walk in the spirit, not in the flesh 5:13-25
    3. Be considerate of the weak and erring 5:26–6:5
  B. General admonitions 6:6-10
    1. Encouragement to support messengers of the gospel 6:6-9
    2. Encouragement to do good to all, especially to believers 6:10

Conclusion 6:11-18

GREETING
(GALATIANS 1:1-5)

1 **Paul, an apostle—sent not from men nor by man, but by Jesus Christ and God the Father, who raised him from the dead—²and all the brothers with me,**

To the churches in Galatia:

³Grace and peace to you from God our Father and the Lord Jesus Christ, ⁴who gave himself for our sins to rescue us from the present evil age, according to the will of our God and Father, ⁵to whom be glory for ever and ever. Amen.

Paul opens his letter according to the normal pattern of his day. There is no complete sentence here; the verses are phrases arranged in a set pattern or formula, consisting of three parts. The ancient author or sender of a letter first would identify himself, together with those who wished to be acknowledged to the readers. Here these are "Paul . . . and all the brothers with me." Then the author would indicate who his intended readers were. This letter was being sent "to the churches in Galatia."

The third part of the formula consisted of greetings or well-wishing, expressed here in the words "grace and peace to you from God our Father and the Lord Jesus Christ." The word for "grace" was the standard Greek word of greeting, and the word for "peace" (shalom) was, and is still, the standard Hebrew greeting. Coming from Paul's pen, however, these words carry an infinitely deeper meaning than that of a common greeting.

Let us take a closer look at each of these three parts of the letter's opening. For convenience we will begin with the second part, the recipients of the letter.

Note that Paul uses the plural when he addresses this letter "to the *churches* in Galatia." As indicated already in the introduction, the assumption we are following is that this is the Roman province of Galatia, located in central Asia Minor, that is, modern Turkey. Paul would have come through this territory on his first missionary journey, about the year A.D. 50. On the outbound portion of that journey he preached in the cities of Antioch, Iconium, Lystra, and Derbe.

He began his preaching efforts in the synagogues, where his gospel message won a number of converts among his Jewish listeners. When the majority of synagogue members turned against him and expelled him from their houses of worship, however, Paul turned to the Gentiles, many of whom gladly heard the message and came to faith in Christ.

On the return portion of his first missionary journey, Paul retraced his steps through these four Galatian cities, setting up a rudimentary organization for the congregations and appointing elders, who were to give enough leadership to keep the preaching and evangelism work going (Acts 14:21-23). Thus the congregations seem to have been made up largely of Gentiles, but with a significant number of Jews, well-versed in the Old Testament Scriptures, serving as elders and spiritual leaders. To these churches the letter to the Galatians was addressed.

The author of the letter is "Paul, an apostle." He needs to say very little about himself because he was well known to them. He was their spiritual father. He had worked among them on his first missionary journey (A.D. 50). About two years later he again came through their territory on his second missionary journey (Acts 16:6). This journey took him beyond Asia Minor into Europe—to the countries of Macedonia and Greece. There in Greece, far separated from his beloved Galatians, word came to Paul about troubles in the Galatian congregations.

As will become clear later in the letter, Paul's person was being attacked in Galatia in an attempt to discredit his message. With his credentials and his authority in question, Paul makes a very significant claim for himself at the outset of his letter. He calls himself "Paul, an *apostle*." An apostle is an ambassador, a representative, someone who has been "sent out" to speak for another. That is the point Paul makes in the opening line of his letter.

He was sent, but "not from men nor by man." To be sure, Paul had been commissioned for foreign mission work by the leaders of the church in Antioch of Syria (Acts 13:1-3). But in the final analysis it was not they who had sent him; nor, for that matter, was he sent by any human authority. Rather, he had been sent "by Jesus Christ and God the Father, who raised him from the dead."

Without going into any detail at this point, Paul reminds the Galatians that he had been personally confronted by Jesus Christ on the road to Damascus. He had been selected by Christ and sent out to preach the gospel. This was not a personal or arbitrary choice by Christ alone. It bore the endorsement also of God the Father who had once and for all indicated his full support of the Son by raising him from the dead. This apostle, chosen by God the Father and God the Son, is the author of the letter to the Galatians. He deserves to be heard—and not only by the Galatians of the first century but by us as well.

He is accompanied by "all the brothers with me." Who these brothers were poses something of a problem. They do not seem to have been Paul's coworkers because Paul usually mentioned these by name. For example, the opening verses of 1 and 2 Corinthians, Philippians, Colossians, 1 and

2 Thessalonians mention such coworkers as Sosthenes, Silas, and Timothy. Nor do the "brothers" seem to have been the believers of the congregation in which Paul was working at the time of writing. These he usually referred to as "saints," literally, "holy ones" (Philippians 4:21,22).

The "brothers" apparently were known to the Galatians, for they needed no introduction. Our assumption is that they may have been a delegation sent to Paul by the Galatians to inform Paul of troubles in their congregation and to request help from him. The letter to the Galatians would then be Paul's response to their request.

We have already alluded to the mixed Jewish and Gentile constituency of the Galatian congregations. Paul's standard Greek greeting, "grace," and its Jewish counterpart, "peace," reflect that mixture. But his words are much more than a standard formula for extending a greeting. For a gospel preacher like Paul, *grace* and *peace* go together as cause and effect.

Grace is that unfathomable quality in God that moves him in Christ to give great and precious gifts to us undeserving sinners. Peace is the effect of grace in our lives.

Paul has both of these qualities in view when in his greeting he speaks of the grace and peace that come "from God our Father and the Lord Jesus Christ, who gave himself for our sins [there's the "grace"] to rescue us from the present evil age [there's the "peace" that comes from sins forgiven]."

Those two elements, grace and peace, lie at the very heart of the gospel. And ironically, it was those two elements that were the object of attack in the Galatian congregations. Small wonder that Paul's agitation showed itself immediately in the introductory paragraph that follows.

INTRODUCTION TO THE LETTER
(GALATIANS 1:6-10)

⁶**I am astonished that you are so quickly deserting the one who called you by the grace of Christ and are turning to a different gospel—⁷which is really no gospel at all. Evidently some people are throwing you into confusion and are trying to pervert the gospel of Christ. ⁸But even if we or an angel from heaven should preach a gospel other than the one we preached to you, let him be eternally condemned! ⁹As we have already said, so now I say again: If anybody is preaching to you a gospel other than what you accepted, let him be eternally condemned!**

¹⁰**Am I now trying to win the approval of men, or of God? Or am I trying to please men? If I were still trying to please men, I would not be a servant of Christ.**

In his other letters Paul normally places what we might call a "laudatory sentence" immediately after the greeting. In this usually long, complex sentence Paul thanks God for the readers' acceptance of the gospel and their growth in faith. Typical is the sentence that begins at Romans 1:8. The third or fourth verse in 1 and 2 Corinthians, Ephesians, Philippians, Colossians, and 1 and 2 Thessalonians also begin with "laudatory sentences." Therefore, it is striking when such a sentence is *not* found in Galatians. Rather, in strong language Paul immediately addresses the problem at hand when he writes, "I am astonished that you are so quickly deserting the one who called you by the grace of Christ and are turning to a different gospel—which is really no gospel at all."

Paul was amazed and astonished that all this was happening so quickly. We are assuming that he had just recently been with them in Galatia at the start of his second missionary journey. He had strengthened them with gospel preaching and teaching. It seemed that all was well, and he moved on to the countries of Macedonia and Greece, where he was now working. But barely had he begun work in the Greek city of Corinth when the bad news came via the delegation of "brothers" from Galatia. The Galatian congregations were deserting the One who had called them by Christ's grace and were turning to a different gospel!

However, Paul has not written off the Galatians. They have not as yet totally and completely rejected the gospel. Paul nonetheless is letting them know they are flirting with something very, very dangerous by listening to a message that plays down grace. He reminds them that it was grace that moved Christ to give himself for their sins and rescue them from the present evil age. They had been rescued, but now they are in danger of reverting to captivity. They had been freed, but now they are toying with the idea of giving up their liberty, yes, of giving up the gospel itself.

What could have led them on so foolhardy a course of action? Paul can draw only one conclusion: "Evidently some people are throwing you into confusion and are trying to pervert the gospel of Christ."

A striking thing about the letter to the Galatians is how little Paul says about the troublemakers. He never names them. He never tells us how many there are, nor even how great their following is. This indicates that Paul's chief concern is for the members of the congregation whose faith is in jeopardy. His heart goes out to them. As a result, Paul doesn't engage in a running battle with the false teachers. In fact, he doesn't address them directly. Rather, he speaks to the congregation about the problem and points out the dangers that beset their faith in Christ.

Paul's analysis of the problem is: "Evidently some people are throwing you into confusion and trying to pervert the gospel of Christ." From hints in the rest of the letter we can conclude to some extent what these troublemakers were up to. Paul regularly warns against accepting the Mosaic Law and submitting to the rite of circumcision. Paul later said the Galatians were beginning to observe "special days and months and seasons and years" (4:10), no doubt a reference to the Jewish Sabbath, the new moon observance, and the annual festivals.

The people causing the confusion seem to have been Judaizers, people who advocated that Gentile Christians enter the kingdom of God by accepting Judaism. These Judaizers did not seem to have denied the merit of Christ's suffering and death. They allowed the necessity of faith in Christ as the promised Savior. Their objection seemed rather to have been directed against the idea of salvation *by faith alone,* because they objected to the thought that salvation can come from God purely as a gift, *by grace alone.* They contended that in addition to accepting Christ, the believer must also keep the Mosaic Law and Old Testament ceremonies.

That was an utter perversion of the free gospel Paul had preached, and he denounces it in the strongest terms. Breathing out a curse, Paul declares: "But even if we or an angel from heaven should preach a gospel other than the one we preached to you, let him be eternally condemned!" He argues that it is really quite unthinkable that he should back off from the message of free grace in Christ he had consistently preached to the Galatians. And if it was *unthinkable* that Paul should deny the grace of Christ, it was utterly *impossible* that an angel would do so. But with a drastic statement Paul shows the seriousness of the situation by saying that even if he or an angel were preaching such a mixture of merit and grace, they should be eternally condemned. Paul does not take false doctrine lightly—as people in our day are inclined to do.

Paul and the angels would not preach such a "gospel" in which human performance was added to Christ's merit, but such preaching was indeed heard in Galatia. Paul doesn't give any names, but he leaves no doubt that he's speaking about his Judaizing opponents when he repeats his curse, "If anybody is preaching to you a gospel other than what you accepted, let him be eternally condemned." Let him be *anathema*. Let him be doomed to hell.

Paul used strong language calculated to silence as quickly as possible the base slander apparently being circulated about him. Paul had a laudable trait that his opponents misunderstood and threw up to him as a fault. In seeking to win converts for the gospel, Paul went out of his way not to offend people or put them off. He himself tells us that he became "all things to all men" (1 Corinthians 9:22). Paul's opponents twisted this around and leveled this charge against him: Paul is just flattering people. He's a clever politician trying to win favor for himself by telling people what they want to hear.

The specific case in point again seems to have involved the observance of the Mosaic Law. Paul did not require his hearers to keep it because it was merely a foreshadowing of Christ, and Christ's coming had rendered it obsolete. The Judaizers, however, still insisted on its observance. In their minds it seemed Paul was letting people off easy by waiving the demands of the law. To them Paul was just buying favor and drawing followers to his cause.

Paul uses his strong *anathema* statement to test his opponents' logic. In view of his drastic curse on the gospel-perverters (verse 9), Paul asks, "Am I now trying to win the approval of men, or of God?" Such action and speech was not calculated to gain the favor of men. Paul resorted to bold speech only to show his loyalty and faithfulness to the One who was his real concern, that is, the God who had called him and given him a message to proclaim. To curry men's favor and turn his back on God would be spiritual suicide, for as Paul says, "If I were still trying to please men [as some claim], I would not be a servant of Christ."

That he is indeed a faithful servant of Christ is the first main point Paul develops in his letter, devoting the remainder of the first and all of the second chapter to that point.

PART ONE
PAUL DEFENDS HIS APOSTLESHIP
(GALATIANS 1:11–2:21)

Paul was called directly by Christ

¹¹I want you to know, brothers, that the gospel I preached is not something that man made up. ¹²I did not receive it from any man, nor was I taught it; rather, I received it by revelation from Jesus Christ.

After his harsh words to the false teachers who were trying to spoil the gospel by mixing human performance with Christ's merits, Paul changes to a warm and winsome tone directed to the congregation members whom he is trying to hearten and encourage in the truth.

Speaking to them as "brothers," he takes up the matter of his relationship to the message he bears. He points out to them at once that it is not his own message. In fact, it's not a human message at all—it's a divine message. It's *God's* Word.

At this point Paul anticipates an objection. Granted, it's God's message, but wasn't it possible that Paul had gotten it from others? For example, had he perhaps received it from the Twelve, who lived and traveled with Jesus, so that he (Paul) was indebted to them for what he knew of the gospel? And if he had learned it from the Twelve, wasn't Paul in a sense a "second-generation" apostle and thus inferior to the "original" apostles?

That is not the case at all, Paul insists. For "I did not receive [the gospel] from *any* man, nor was I taught it; rather, I received it by revelation from Jesus Christ."

The gospel of free salvation by grace was not the kind of message that men would devise, so it could not be received from any human source. Nor was Paul a particularly docile or teachable sort of person, easily brought to a new point of view. No, as he himself will point out shortly, he violently resisted any changes in his religious views. The only thing that could adequately account for Paul's acceptance of the gospel was that he had received this message directly from Christ, by revelation.

So important is this point to Paul's presentation that he bolsters his claim of direct revelation from Christ with four supporting arguments:

1. His life before conversion (verses 13,14);
2. The circumstances surrounding his conversion at Damascus (verses 15-17);
3. His visit to Jerusalem three years after conversion (verses 18-20);
4. His stay in Syria and Cilicia (verses 21-24).

Paul's life before his conversion

13For you have heard of my previous way of life in Judaism, how intensely I persecuted the church of God and tried to destroy it. 14I was advancing in Judaism beyond many Jews of my own age and was extremely zealous for the traditions of my fathers.

Note that verse 13 opens with "for." It's giving a reason; this verse is lending support to a previous statement. Paul had emphasized that he did not get his gospel from men. To this he adds another argument: If you know the circumstances of my case, it's really very unlikely that I would be influenced by men. I was the kind of fellow to whom nobody could tell anything. Just look at my track record.

"You have heard of my previous way of life in Judaism, how intensely I persecuted the church." How had the Galatians heard? No doubt Paul had told them. We know that in other instances Paul did not shirk from disclosing the details of his sordid past. He told the Corinthians that he didn't deserve to be called an apostle "because I persecuted the church of God" (1 Corinthians 15:9), and to Timothy he admitted, "I was once a blasphemer and a persecutor and a violent man" (1 Timothy 1:13). In all likelihood Paul was just as open with the Galatians. At any rate, they had heard of his way of life in Judaism.

Nor are we left in the dark regarding Paul's record as a persecutor. The book of Acts gives us a clear and graphic picture. We first meet Paul as a young man guarding the clothes of those who threw the stones in the execution of Stephen, the first Christian martyr.

From this role of *passive* alignment with Jewish opposition to Christianity, we soon find Paul as a very *active* persecutor of Christians. It would be hard to improve on Paul's own description of that anti-Christian activity. At his trial before Agrippa, Paul said:

> I . . . was convinced that I ought to do all that was possible to oppose the name of Jesus of Nazareth. And that is just what I did in Jerusalem. On the authority of the chief priests I put many of the saints in prison, and when they were put to death, I cast my vote against them. Many a time I went from one synagogue to another to have them punished, and I tried to force them to blaspheme. In my obsession against them, I even went to foreign cities to persecute them (Acts 26:9-11).

There was no sign of Paul's letting up in his zeal for the tradition of his fathers. He was successful in the program; he was advancing in Judaism beyond many of his contemporaries. Under those circumstances, there was no chance that anyone could talk him out of Judaism or persuade him to accept for himself the Christian faith that he was so zealously and successfully persecuting. No human being could budge Paul, but when God spoke, he paid attention.

Circumstances surrounding Paul's conversion

¹⁵But when God, who set me apart from birth and called me by his grace, was pleased ¹⁶to reveal his Son in me so that I might preach him among the Gentiles, I did not consult any man, ¹⁷nor did I go up to Jerusalem to see those who were apostles before I was, but I went immediately into Arabia and later returned to Damascus.

Keep in mind the point of Paul's argument in this section. He is establishing the fact that his apostleship in no way depended upon man's doing. Thus the key words of the verse are in the last clause of verse 16, where Paul says, "I did not consult any man."

Men did not make Paul an apostle or influence him to become one. It was wholly God's doing. Paul drives home that thought with four verbal ideas: "God . . . set me apart . . . called me . . . revealed his Son . . . so that I might preach him." Each of these deserves a bit of comment.

Paul says, "God . . . set me apart from birth." Note that before there could be any human influence on Paul, in fact, before he was even born, God already knew all about Paul. In his infinite wisdom God had chosen him; he had set him apart to be an apostle.

What God in eternity purposed to do, he carried out in time when he "called me by his grace," as Paul says. We know, of course, what the circumstances were when God called Paul. Paul was on his way to Damascus, bent on his terrible mission of hunting down God's children, the Christians. One might have expected God to be violently angry with Paul. We can even picture to ourselves how God in his just wrath might have been inclined to snuff out Paul's life—the way we might slap an offending mosquito.

But no, instead of showing fierce anger, God in his great grace "was pleased to reveal his Son in me." That too is a familiar account, the details of which need not detain us. Simply recall that when the bright light appeared and Paul was knocked down on the roadway, he heard the curt question "Saul, Saul, why do you persecute me?" (Acts 9:4).

To Paul's frightened question, "Who are you?" came this answer: "I am Jesus, whom you are persecuting. . . . Now get up and go into the city, and you will be told what you must do" (Acts 9:5,6). Paul's mission was conveyed to him in Damascus by God's messenger Ananias. Paul was to "preach [Christ] among the Gentiles."

In all this it was clear that *God* had ordained Paul as an apostle. God called him and revealed Christ to him. He commissioned Paul as an apostle to the Gentiles. God had spoken, and it would have ill-befitted Paul at this stage to ask for human advice as to what he was supposed to do about God's directive to him.

In fact, Paul did not even seek the opinion of those whom he might have been expected to consult, namely the Christians whose cause he was about to join. Rather, Paul says, "[I did not] go up to Jerusalem to see those who were apostles before I was."

Paul did not consult with anyone. He didn't need to because he was sure of his message. After all, it had come directly from the risen Christ—just as had the message the apostles in Jerusalem were preaching. Nor did Paul check out his gospel with the apostles. The messages of both were in agreement. Consequently, Paul was not inclined to go back to Jerusalem but, as he says, "I went immediately into Arabia and later returned to Damascus."

From his lodging place in Damascus Paul headed for Arabia. With our modern sense of geography we may be inclined to associate the term "Arabia" with the triangular peninsula far to the southwest of Damascus—the area today occupied mainly by Saudi Arabia. In ancient times, however, territory bearing the name "Arabia" extended much farther north. In fact, one or two days' journey eastward from Damascus would have brought Paul into the territory known as Stony Arabia.

More difficult than the matter of location is the question of what Paul did in Arabia. Scripture does not answer the question, so we are left to surmise. Some have suggested that Paul preached the gospel there. Stony Arabia, however, was thinly populated and an unlikely place in which to do mission work. To this writer it seems more plausible that Paul withdrew to this quiet area in order to meditate and to work through the Scriptures. To be sure, as a devout Jewish Pharisee Paul knew the content of the Old Testament well, but he had never really understood it because he failed to see Christ in it. In the dramatic confrontation on the road to Damascus and the accompanying revelation of Christ, Paul received the key to the Old Testament. Now everything fell into place, the more so as Paul reworked familiar passages, which now took on new meaning.

If these days in Arabia were a time in which Paul sorted things out in connection with his understanding of the Old Testament, it would be understandable that he would come back to Damascus a much-improved and strengthened proclaimer of the Christian message. Luke seems to agree with that when he describes Paul's activity in Damascus with the words "Yet Saul grew more and more powerful and baffled the Jews living in Damascus by proving that Jesus is the Christ" (Acts 9:22).

Paul's visit to Jerusalem three years after conversion

[18]Then after three years, I went up to Jerusalem to get acquainted with Peter and stayed with him fifteen days. [19]I saw none of the other apostles—only James, the Lord's brother. [20]I assure you before God that what I am writing you is no lie.

When we remember that all along Paul's point has been that he was called to be an apostle directly by God, without any human intervention, we easily see the thrust of every statement that Paul builds into this section.

Paul has informed us that his immediate reaction was not to go to Jerusalem, but rather to withdraw to the solitude of Arabia and from there to return to Damascus for more gospel work. He now informs us that he stayed in Damascus for a considerable period of time. In fact, it wasn't until three years later that he decided to go to Jerusalem. And when he did go, it was not to receive instruction or approval for his message. Rather, he went to get acquainted with the great apostle Peter.

Even if he had intended to receive information from Peter, the time Paul spent with him was really too short to launch into anything like a course of study, for Paul tells the Galatians that he stayed with Peter only 15 days.

So much for Peter. But did Paul perhaps come under the influence of the other apostles? Paul says, "I saw none of the other apostles—only James, the Lord's brother." Paul's point is crystal clear. He received no input from the other apostles because none of them were in town. The only one he saw was James, the Lord's brother.

Paul seems to be using the term "apostle" in the wider sense here. This James was not one of the Twelve but was one of Jesus' brothers, mentioned at various places in Scripture. At first these brothers did not have a proper understanding of Jesus' mission and ministry, and they did not put their trust in him as a spiritual savior (John 7:1-5).

Soon after Christ's resurrection, however, we find his brothers a recognizable group solidly associated with the faithful followers of Christ. The opening chapter of Acts, for example, enumerates the names of the Twelve (minus Judas Iscariot) and says of them, "They all joined together constantly in prayer, along with the women and Mary the mother of Jesus, *and with his brothers.*" Obviously, Jesus' brothers had become believers.

Although Scripture does not specifically relate it, a solid block of tradition says that after the departure of the Twelve to carry out their worldwide mission assignment, James the brother of our Lord became the acknowledged head of the Christian church in Jerusalem. Paul, in chapter 2, verse 9, refers to James as a pillar of the Jerusalem church.

Paul acknowledges that he met James but that he too played no part in making or approving Paul's apostleship. Just how sensitive was the issue of Paul's apostleship is evident from Paul's next statement. With an oath Paul declares, "I assure you before God that what I am writing you is no lie." From this strong disclaimer it is clear that reports were circulating among the Galatians alleging Paul's dependence on the original apostles of Christ and hence his inferiority to them. Since the trustworthiness and reliability of Paul's gospel message are at stake, he dare not let the disparaging reports go unchecked.

Paul's stay in Syria and Cilicia

²¹Later I went to Syria and Cilicia. ²²I was personally unknown to the churches of Judea that are in Christ. ²³They only heard the report: "The man who formerly persecuted us is now preaching the faith he once tried to destroy." ²⁴And they praised God because of me.

In the previous section we left Paul in Jerusalem, to which he had come from Damascus. Now he continues, "Later I went to Syria and Cilicia." His stay in Jerusalem sounds quiet and peaceful enough, but from the account in Acts it doesn't seem to have been all that tranquil. In Acts 9:28-30 we read, "Saul stayed with [the apostles] and moved about freely in Jerusalem, speaking boldly in the name of the Lord. He talked and debated with the Grecian Jews, but they tried to kill him. When the brothers learned of this, they took him down to Caesarea and sent him off to Tarsus." (See also Acts 22:17-21.) For his own safety Paul was whisked out of Jerusalem and sent to his home in the city of Tarsus, located in the country of Cilicia. "Syria" is simply the Roman provincial name for that whole northern territory.

Piecing together the details and dates of Paul's life poses some problems, but by looking at what information and datable incidents we do have, it is possible to calculate that Paul's stay in Tarsus may have been somewhat longer than his low-key reference here would suggest. He could have been there as long as seven or eight years.

Whatever the specific length of time Paul spent in Tarsus, the point of mentioning his stay there is still the same. Paul was far away from where the other apostles conducted their activity. He didn't need to be in touch with them. He was an apostle in his own right, called directly by God. Hence it was

31

of no concern to him that he was personally unknown to the Christian churches in Judea.

Up to this point Paul's argumentation has been dwelling on the negative aspect of his relationship to the rest of the established church—his detachment from it. But now the chapter ends on a gloriously positive tone.

While the Christian churches of Judea did not personally know Paul, they kept hearing good things about him. The consistent report was, "The man who formerly persecuted us is now preaching the faith he once tried to destroy." Even though Paul was not part of the Judean establishment, he was preaching the very same Christian message they were hearing from the original apostles. This unity in doctrine and faith gave the Judean Christians great joy, and they praised God for it.

This aspect of unity in doctrine and faith forms an excellent bridge for Paul to lead into the second chapter of his letter to the Galatians.

Paul was received by the other apostles

Apparently in Galatia Paul was suffering attacks from his opponents that went something like this: "Paul is not one of Christ's original apostles. He's a Johnny-come-lately to the scene. Hence you can't be sure that he has it all straight. For example, when he urges freedom from the Mosaic Law, he's going against what Jewish teachers have always taught."

Paul's argument up to this point has been that he didn't need to be closely associated with the Jerusalem apostles because he was just like them—a full-fledged apostle, called directly by God. Therefore, he didn't need any human bolstering or support.

Paul's new emphasis, sustained throughout the second chapter, is that while he did not need any human support or undergirding for his apostleship, when he did come into contact with the Jerusalem apostles they wholeheartedly accepted him and the doctrine he taught. To illustrate and prove that he was indeed received as a brother and fellow apostle, Paul draws on three major incidents:

1. His gospel was recognized at the Jerusalem Council (verses 1-5);
2. An area of gospel work was accorded to him (verses 6-10);
3. Peter accepted Paul's admonition (verses 11-21).

Paul's gospel was recognized at the Jerusalem Council

2 **Fourteen years later I went up again to Jerusalem, this time with Barnabas. I took Titus along also. ²I went in response to a revelation and set before them the gospel that I preach among the Gentiles. But I did this privately to those who seemed to be leaders, for fear that I was running or had run my race in vain. ³Yet not even Titus, who was with me, was compelled to be circumcised, even though he was a Greek.**

Note once more the length of time during which Paul had no contact with Jerusalem. During a good portion of this time Paul was in Syria and Cilicia. Now, 14 years later, he returned to Jerusalem.

Some understand this to be 14 years after Paul's conversion, just as the "three years" of verse 18 used Paul's conversion as its starting point. Those who follow that reckoning then say that the visit referred to here was the one Acts 11:25-30 brings to our attention. There Paul and Barnabas went up to Jerusalem to deliver a gift to needy Jewish Christians suffering in a famine.

The view favored by this writer is that the 14 years have as their starting point Paul's previously mentioned visit to

Jerusalem, or 17 years after his conversion. This would make it more likely that the reference is to Paul's attending the "Jerusalem Council."

The main reasons for this choice are that the "famine visit" to Jerusalem was apparently brief, not at all controversial, and, above all, without any bearing on the problem of Judaizers that Paul is dealing with in his letter to the Galatians.

On the other hand, the Jerusalem Council, held about A.D. 51, devoted itself entirely to the problem of the Judaizers. So much are they the focus of attention that one can hardly imagine Paul not referring to the council rather extensively in this present letter, which was sent to deal with a very similar problem.

An understanding of the circumstances surrounding the Jerusalem Council is useful to a proper understanding of the Judaizers and their way of thinking. So it will be worth our while to review Acts 15.

Luke describes the situation very graphically. After Paul had finished his first missionary journey, he returned to Antioch in Syria, to the church that had commissioned him and Barnabas. There they reported on the success of their mission, pointing to the conversion of many Gentiles and stating very frankly that they had been accepted into membership in the Christian church on the basis of their confession of faith and trust in Christ, without their promising to adhere to the Mosaic Law.

The Antioch congregation was delighted, but Paul's law-free gospel soon drew sparks from a different quarter. Luke reports in Acts 15:1-5:

> Some men came down from Judea to Antioch and were teaching the brothers: "Unless you are circumcised, according to the custom taught by

Moses, you cannot be saved." This brought Paul and Barnabas into sharp dispute and debate with them. So Paul and Barnabas were appointed, along with some other believers, to go up to Jerusalem to see the apostles and elders about this question. The church sent them on their way, and as they traveled through Phoenicia and Samaria, they told how the Gentiles had been converted. This news made all the brothers very glad. When they came to Jerusalem, they were welcomed by the church and the apostles and elders, to whom they reported everything God had done through them.

Then some of the believers who belonged to the party of the Pharisees stood up and said, "The Gentiles must be circumcised and required to obey the law of Moses."

Note how clearly the issue comes into focus, both in Antioch and again in Jerusalem. Against Paul's law-free gospel the Judaizers insisted: "Faith in Christ isn't enough. The Gentiles must *also* be circumcised and agree to keep the Law of Moses if they expect to be saved."

This was the same issue under contention in Galatia, and the outcome of this earlier meeting in Jerusalem would surely be important to Paul and would enter into any discussion or letter that Paul might send the Galatians.*

---

*For this reason, and because of the obvious parallelism between Acts 15 and the opening verses of Paul's second chapter to the Galatians, it is our feeling that the Council at Jerusalem, and not the famine visit, is being referred to here.

We need to take into consideration a few differences from the Acts 15 account, however. First of all is the matter of Titus' presence, mentioned in Galatians but not in Acts. Recall, however, that Luke in Acts reports that the congregation delegated Paul and Barnabas "along with some other believers" to go to Jerusalem. Titus would seem to fit there.

Furthermore, Paul in Galatians speaks of going up to Jerusalem *by revelation*. That might seem to suggest the famine visit since Acts says that on that occasion

What was the outcome of the Jerusalem Council? That decision would be of tremendous consequence for the parallel situation in Galatia. Paul says, "Yet not even Titus, who was with me, was compelled to be circumcised, even though he was a Greek."

At the Jerusalem Council as well as in Galatia, the issue was whether or not the Gentiles were free from the ceremonies commanded in the Mosaic law. Titus was a Greek, a non-Jew, a Gentile. But he was not compelled to be circumcised. The Jerusalem Council agreed completely with Paul and his teaching that salvation comes purely by grace, as a gift, to those who believe and trust in Christ—without any deeds of the law. In fact, the Jerusalem Christians would never have brought the matter up. Rather, the problem stemmed from a different source, as Paul informs us:

⁴This matter arose because some false brothers had infiltrated our ranks to spy on the freedom we have in Christ Jesus and to make us slaves. ⁵We did not give in to them for a moment, so that the truth of the gospel might remain with you.

All the apostles were in agreement regarding salvation by faith alone as a free gift from God. The idea of adding works

---

Paul went up to Jerusalem as a result of a revelation to Agabus (Acts 11:27-30), but nothing rules out the possibility that God gave Paul specific instruction by revelation also for the Jerusalem Council. That Luke in Acts 15 doesn't mention it doesn't prove that it didn't happen.

Finally, there is the matter of Paul telling the Galatians that he presented the matter *privately* to the leaders, while Acts speaks of an open meeting. Here too, one does not rule out the other. Consider the manner in which things are done at our synod conventions. Virtually no business is presented to the general assembly without prior discussion. The matter is first assigned to a floor committee (private discussion) for subsequent presentation in the open meeting. The two fit together very naturally. So too, Galatians and Acts are not at odds with each other. One stresses the private, the other the public aspect of the meeting.

came from "false brothers." Take another look at the trouble-makers in Jerusalem, as described in Acts 15. Luke says, "Some of the believers who belonged to the party of the Pharisees stood up and said, 'The Gentiles must be circumcised and required to obey the law of Moses.'"

They claimed to be believers in Christ, but they said some thoroughly unchristian things. In fact, they were really nothing other than adherents to the party of the Pharisees when they insisted that Jewish ceremonies had to be observed for salvation. Thus, they were Judaizers.

Such people "infiltrated" the Christian congregation with the express purpose of taking away the free gift of salvation. They would have reduced people to the status of slaves by making them *work* for what Christ died to *give* them.

It was a dangerous situation, both at the Jerusalem Council and also in Galatia. Such teaching was a corruption of the gospel and would deprive its adherents of their salvation, for it would make them totally dependent on themselves by robbing them of Christ's merit. Hence Paul tells the Galatians, "We did not give in to them for a moment, so that the truth of the gospel might remain with you."

The error of mixing faith and works had been successfully withstood in Jerusalem. Paul's teaching had been completely vindicated. But that was not merely a personal victory for Paul, a feather in his cap. No, the apostles' firmness against the false teachers had retained the gospel—for the benefit of the Galatians. And in order that the law-free gospel agreed upon in Jerusalem might now remain with the Galatians, Paul begs them not to listen to his opponents whose message was very similar to that of the "false brothers" in Jerusalem. Rather, he urges the Galatians to accept the testimony of the apostles, who had totally agreed with Paul's teaching that no ceremonies or works were to be required for salvation.

An area of gospel work was accorded to Paul

⁶**As for those who seemed to be important—whatever they were makes no difference to me; God does not judge by external appearance—those men added nothing to my message. ⁷On the contrary, they saw that I had been entrusted with the task of preaching the gospel to the Gentiles, just as Peter had been to the Jews. ⁸For God, who was at work in the ministry of Peter as an apostle to the Jews, was also at work in my ministry as an apostle to the Gentiles. ⁹James, Peter and John, those reputed to be pillars, gave me and Barnabas the right hand of fellowship when they recognized the grace given to me. They agreed that we should go to the Gentiles, and they to the Jews. ¹⁰All they asked was that we should continue to remember the poor, the very thing I was eager to do.**

Paul remains aware of the fact that much of his argumentation to this point has been stressing his independence from the Jerusalem apostles. He has been contending that he is an apostle not by their authorization or support, but because God called him. He retains this emphasis by asserting that whatever external role or station in life the Jerusalem apostles held makes no difference. God does not judge by such a standard, nor does it affect the validity of the judgment reached at the Jerusalem Council. Those who were deemed important in Jerusalem weren't critical of Paul nor did they add anything to his message.

Not only did they find no fault with Paul's message, but they recognized that he was preaching the same gospel as Peter and the rest of the Jerusalem apostles. Both were building the kingdom by preaching the same message. The only difference was the people to whom they were preaching.

They saw that the preaching of Peter and the Jerusalem apostles had been singularly blessed in its effect upon Jews, whereas Paul was preaching the gospel with amazing results to Gentiles. There was unity in their doctrine and equality in their respective apostleships.

Hence there was really only one thing to do: recognize and acknowledge openly the facts of the case. Paul reports: "James, Peter and John, those reputed to be pillars, gave me and Barnabas the right hand of fellowship when they recognized the grace given to me. They agreed that we should go to the Gentiles, and they to the Jews."

Giving the right hand of fellowship didn't establish anything new. It recognized what was already in existence and was a token of acceptance and equality. With a handshake they agreed that Paul and Barnabas should continue to go to the Gentiles, while Peter and his associates would serve the Jews.

It should perhaps be noted that this division was not intended to be hard and fast. It was not a staking out of territory and daring the other to cross. There were always exceptions on both sides.

For example, on Paul's second missionary journey, which followed shortly after the Jerusalem Council, he continued his pattern of going first to the Jewish synagogue when he came to a new place (Acts 17:2). He preached in the synagogue as long as the Jews would tolerate him. Usually that wasn't very long, and after being expelled from the synagogue, Paul would spend the bulk of his time working with Gentiles.

On the other hand, recall that Peter, the prime representative of gospel preaching to the Jews, didn't restrict his ministry exclusively to Jews either. To be sure, the opening chapters of Acts speak predominantly of Peter's work with Jews in and around Jerusalem. But Peter also went to the Samaritans who were at best only half Jewish (Acts 8:14-25). And God himself very formally directed Peter to go to Cornelius, who was a full Gentile (Acts 10). Furthermore, there seem to be good and valid reasons for concluding that Peter's epistles, written toward the end of his life, were addressed to Gentiles.

The handshake in Jerusalem was not restrictive. It didn't keep either party from preaching the gospel as opportunity arose. What it indicated, rather, was that Peter and Paul were agreed on the gospel that was to be preached. Each of them was a full-fledged apostle, and one acknowledged the other as an equal.

That point was important for the Galatians. They had been fed stories about Paul's dependence on and inferiority to the Jerusalem apostles. The implication was that Paul didn't have the message straight and was preaching something else to Gentiles from what Peter was preaching to Jews. Not true! says Paul.

There was total understanding and agreement between the Jewish and Gentile branches of the Christian church. Both were to hear the message of salvation by faith in Christ without the requirement of any ceremonies or works. And to give tangible evidence of the spiritual, and thus invisible, unity that existed between Jewish and Gentile Christians, a charitable program was agreed upon. Paul says, "All they asked was that we should continue to remember the poor, the very thing I was eager to do." Again, this was not really something new. If we are right in assuming that this is taking place at the Jerusalem Council, then Paul and Barnabas' famine visit of Acts 11 would have been some three years earlier. And that fits in nicely with the description here. Paul and Barnabas are asked to "continue to remember" the poor, as they had indeed done in the past.

Peter accepts Paul's admonition

As a representative of the Christian church in Jerusalem, Peter had given Paul the right hand of fellowship, thereby indicating acceptance and equality. This expression of fellowship was a relatively easy step to take. The real test, however, would come when that arrangement was applied to the realities of everyday life. What would happen if Paul and Peter had a difference of opinion? Who would win out if they ever crossed paths? Paul tells us that actually did happen. A tense and stressful confrontation arose between the two men—and Peter yielded!

We need to remain very clear as to Paul's motives here. Paul was not building up his own ego, but advancing and defending the gospel message to which both he and Peter had agreed at the Council of Jerusalem. In the following section Paul points out that this gospel message saved the day in an unhappy confrontation he had with Peter in Antioch and that this very same gospel message is what Paul is now defending against a similar attack in Galatia.

¹¹When Peter came to Antioch, I opposed him to his face, because he was clearly in the wrong. ¹²Before certain men came from James, he used to eat with the Gentiles. But when they arrived, he began to draw back and separate himself from the Gentiles because he was afraid of those who belonged to the circumcision group. ¹³The other Jews joined him in his hypocrisy, so that by their hypocrisy even Barnabas was led astray.

"Antioch" was not that city in Asia Minor evangelized by Paul and Barnabas on their first missionary journey but Antioch on the Orontes River, located several hundred miles north of Jerusalem on the border between modern Turkey and Syria. It was a mixed congregation, one of the earliest containing both Jews and Gentiles (Acts 11:19-26). It was the congregation from which Paul and Barnabas were commissioned at the outset of their Gentile mission work, and it always remained the "base" from which they carried on subsequent outreach efforts. In a way, Antioch became the mother church for Gentiles, as Jerusalem was for Jewish Christians. It is not surprising, therefore, that in the course of Peter's travels he would visit this great center of Christianity and associate with Antioch's mixed constituency of Jews and Gentiles.

The gospel, with its message of Christian liberty, had apparently made things very relaxed in Antioch. The Antioch Christians realized that no human work or merit was necessary for salvation. So no special emphasis was placed either on the observance or the non-observance of Jewish ceremonies. If Jewish Christians preferred to eat "kosher" at the fellowship meals, that was fine. Or if they wished to enjoy a pork chop or a ham sandwich with their Gentile fellow Christians, that was permissible also. Peter, we're told, "used to eat with the Gentiles." He didn't strictly observe the traditional Jewish patterns. But that was "before certain men came from James."

We have stated that James, the brother of our Lord, became the dominant figure in the Jerusalem church. So prominent was he, in fact, that his name became virtually synonymous with Jerusalem. Hence we needn't conclude that James necessarily sent them; rather, some men from James' area of administration showed up in Antioch while Peter was there.

It's likely that Peter wasn't concerned about James, whose position on Gentile liberty he knew well from the Jerusalem Council. Nor was he particularly concerned about those who had come from Jerusalem. Peter's real concern, unfortunately, seems to have been based on a fear of what difficulties and unpleasantness might result for him if word of his eating with Gentiles got back to a troublesome element in Jerusalem. In short, "he was afraid of those who belonged to the circumcision group." Call them Judaizers, if you will.

We have already noted what problems they caused Paul—problems that required the convening of a special council at Jerusalem. Nor had Peter been spared their criticism. They complained bitterly about his entering the home of the Gentile Cornelius and eating with them (Acts 11:1-3). On that occasion Peter gave these "circumcised believers," as Acts labels them, a very straightforward, gospel-centered answer.

Unfortunately, he did less well here in Antioch. He quietly withdrew from his former open association with Gentiles. He again began to eat kosher at the get-togethers. He mingled with the Jewish Christians and reverted to Jewish customs.

Such an example didn't go unnoticed. Other Jewish Christians followed his lead. Eventually even Barnabas, Paul's great companion in mission outreach to the Gentiles, felt the pressure and changed his pattern. These men knew better, but they caved in to Peter's example. It was, as Paul called it, "hypocrisy" and required immediate and firm action. Paul states:

¹⁴**When I saw that they were not acting in line with the truth of the gospel, I said to Peter in front of them all, "You are a Jew, yet you live like a Gentile and not like a Jew. How is it, then, that you force Gentiles to follow Jewish customs?"**

Note the seriousness of the situation. These people were "not acting in line with the truth of the gospel." This was soul-destroying error rearing its head. This teaching endangered people's salvation. Furthermore, Peter's example had been given in public. His conduct affected them all and put pressure on everyone. As the teaching had been public, so the correction also had to be public. Hence Paul addresses Peter individually and in front of them all, pointing out the contradictory nature of his actions.

Peter was a Jew, yet at his coming to Antioch he had initially moved very freely in Gentile circles, even eating with them. Thereby he illustrated the gospel principle that Jewish customs and ceremonies had no inherent worth. They need not be observed as requirements for salvation.

By changing his procedure, however, Peter was denying that former principle. He was now acting as though living a Gentile lifestyle was injurious to a person's chances for salvation—as though observing Jewish custom or keeping the Mosaic Law really did help to improve one's relationship to God after all. Thus by his example Peter was forcing Gentiles "to follow Jewish customs."

With our growing awareness of the evils of bias and discrimination against ethnic groups, we have developed an aversion to the idea of one group forcing its culture or customs on another. We hear much about the dignity of each individual as a person and the inherent worth of his or her ethnic culture. Note, however, that Paul does *not* follow such logic here. Paul is not downplaying Jewish customs because he wants to uphold Gentile culture. (Later he will have some negative things to say about their culture.) As important as cultural concerns are, Paul's objection here rests on quite a different basis. His point is that before God no human work or activity has any merit. Even Jewish customs and ceremonies have no value for salvation. To force them on the Gentiles is not a cultural crime, but a spiritual one. It undermines the gospel. Speaking as a Jew to a fellow Jew, Paul tells Peter:

[15]**"We who are Jews by birth and not 'Gentile sinners' [16]know that a man is not justified by observing the law, but by faith in Jesus Christ. So we, too, have put our faith in Christ Jesus that we may be justified by faith in Christ and not by observing the law, because by observing the law no one will be justified."**

The Jews had many advantages. They were, after all, God's chosen people whom he had taken into a special covenant relationship with himself. Because of this relationship God, through Moses, had given the Jews many regulations and directives to guide them in their everyday lives and worship.

But the Jews who truly understood the nature of this covenant with God never trusted or relied on their performance of these special regulations as the reason why God should be gracious to them. For example, when they brought their sacrifices, it was not viewed as something they did for God; their sacrifices served, rather, as reminders of God's great promise. The sacrifices of an ox or lamb foreshadowed the real Sacrifice that God had promised to make for them—the Lamb of God, who as the Savior of the world would one day suffer and die in their place.

When they were properly understood, all the Mosaic ceremonies and customs were viewed as a teaching medium—a reminder of the promised Messiah, the Christ who was to come. And the preparatory role and the teaching nature of these regulations became even clearer after Christ appeared and declared himself to be the fulfillment of all these Old Testament foreshadowings. Hence Paul expects Peter to agree with him when he says, "We . . . know that a man is not justified by observing the law, but by faith in Jesus Christ."

In effect, Paul is saying to his fellow apostle who was pressuring the Gentiles to keep the Old Testament ceremonies: "Come on, Peter! Even we Jews don't trust in our keeping of Moses' ordinances and ceremonies, because we know that our salvation rests solely on Christ's merit. And if even we to whom the law was given don't rely on it for our salvation, why should we pressure Gentiles to keep it?" The folly, yes even the danger, in urging people to keep the Mosaic Law lay in their being led to put trust and confidence in their obedience and assumed merit. They would then be trusting in something that couldn't save them, for as Paul adds, "By observing the law no one will be justified."

That thought will receive a great deal more attention in the third and fourth chapters of the letter. Meanwhile, Paul anticipates another objection and heads it off. Still speaking to Peter he says:

[17]"If, while we seek to be justified in Christ, it becomes evident that we ourselves are sinners, does that mean that Christ promotes sin? Absolutely not! [18]If I rebuild what I destroyed, I prove that I am a lawbreaker."

To understand this verse we must realize that the sense in which Paul uses the word "sinners" is not the same as the sense in which he uses the word "sin." That may require some explanation.

Recall that in the previous section Paul spoke of Peter and himself as "Jews by birth" and not "Gentile sinners." The term "sinner" was a common derogatory term Jews attached to Gentiles. The Gentiles' chief "sin," of course, was that they did not observe the Mosaic Law. They ate unclean foods, worked on the Sabbath, didn't offer sacrifices, didn't circumcise their sons, etc.

Paul has just finished saying that the believer in Christ is justified, that is, rendered acceptable before God. Observing the Mosaic Law makes no difference at all for justification. The law may fairly be disregarded, as Peter himself disregarded it initially upon his arrival at Antioch. But by standard Jewish terminology nonobservance of the Mosaic Law made people "sinners." By trusting in Christ and not their observance of the Mosaic Law, Christian Jews really became "sinners" in the sense in which that term was regularly hung on the Gentiles.

Paul now asks the question, "Is this 'nonobservance' of the Mosaic Law a real, moral wrongdoing, a 'sin,' in the proper sense of the term? Or, to take it a step farther, if faith in Christ allows people to disregard the law, could one say that Christ is a promoter of sin?" "Absolutely not!" Paul replies.

Quite the opposite is true. Upholding the Mosaic Law and advocating it (as Peter did in weakness and as the Judaizers in Galatia were doing by design and conviction) is the real sin; that makes a person a lawbreaker. That is criminal, because it spoils the gospel and robs men of the free gift of salvation. Hence the apostle asserts, "If I rebuild what I destroyed [the Mosaic Law], I prove that I am a lawbreaker."

Paul's tact at this point is rather striking. Note that he shifts to the first person. By turning to his own case he is, in a sense, taking the heat off Peter and his unfortunate building up of the Mosaic Law. Paul himself had made the same mistake. Paul had gone the route of legalism. He had been a Pharisee, bent on serving God with such fervor that he'd become acceptable to God. But it didn't work. He could impress men, but not God. God himself had to confront him on the road to Damascus and tell him that what he was doing in trying to earn God's favor was totally wrong. It had to be wrong because, as Paul subsequently learned to say, "By observing the law no one will be justified." It lies in the nature of the case that no one can be justified by deeds of law, because no one can do God's will perfectly.

[19]"For through the law I died to the law so that I might live for God. [20]I have been crucified with Christ and I no longer live, but Christ lives in me. The life I live in the body, I live by faith in the Son of God, who loved me and gave himself for me. [21]I do not set aside the grace of God, for if righteousness could be gained through the law, Christ died for nothing!"

47

Notice the tone of hopelessness and helplessness that shows through when Paul says, "For through the law I died to the law." Yet dying to the law and despairing of his own ability had a very wholesome effect on Paul. It drove home to him the impossibility of earning salvation by himself and made very attractive the only possible alternative, letting someone else meet God's just demands for him. Then Paul became willing to accept the gospel, which brought him the good news that Christ had done everything for him.

By faith Paul shares in Christ's merit. In fact, so close is his connection with Christ that Paul can say he has been "crucified with Christ." It really is no longer Paul who is living, but Christ who lives in him. "The life I live in the body, I live by faith in the Son of God, who loved me and gave himself for me."

Not the demands of any law, but love for the Savior was moving Paul to live the life of willing obedience he now leads. Only such a life, motivated by love and gratitude, is consistent with the gospel of free grace in Christ. For if righteousness could be gained through our obedience—if justification really depended to some extent on our observing laws—then Christ's death for us would have been in vain.

With these words Paul concludes his rebuke to Peter, and on this note he also closes the first part of his letter to the Galatians. Recall the emphasis throughout this opening section. Paul was being challenged by Judaizers who questioned his authority in view of the fact that he was not one of the original apostles, who followed Christ during his public ministry and then were formally commissioned at his ascension. Paul's response was that he needed no connection to the Jerusalem apostles because he was their equal in every way, since he too had been called by God and formally commissioned to preach the gospel.

To support this claim of equality Paul marshaled three proofs: At the Jerusalem Council the original apostles found no fault with his teaching of a law-free gospel, for Titus was not required to observe any Old Testament ceremonies. Furthermore, the Jerusalem apostles acknowledged the trustworthiness and reliability of the message Paul preached, for they encouraged him and Barnabas to continue preaching that gospel to the Gentiles while they would continue to share the same message with Jews. Finally, when Peter later in Antioch unfortunately departed from the message both sides had agreed on, he recognized the validity of Paul's rebuke and accepted the correction Paul offered.

Thus, it is evident from Paul's line of logic that both he and the Jerusalem apostles were preaching the same gospel. But just what was the gospel they were preaching? And what is the relationship of the Old Testament ceremonies to the New Testament gospel? That will be the thrust of the second main part of Paul's letter. Here Paul will address himself to the doctrine of justification, that very important topic of how a gross and vile sinner can be accepted by a just and holy God.

"Does God give you his Spirit and work miracles among you because you observe the law, or because you believe what you heard?" (3:5)

PART TWO
PAUL EXPLAINS JUSTIFICATION—
HOW THE SINNER BECOMES
ACCEPTED BEFORE GOD
(GALATIANS 3:1–4:31)

Not by works, but by faith alone

In Paul's letter to the Galatians there has been and will continue to be a great deal of discussion about Jewish ceremonies and the Law of Moses. That is only natural when we recall the problem in Galatia. Judaizers were urging Gentile Christians to make their salvation certain by conforming their lives and actions to the Jewish way.

The fundamental error was telling people to do something in order to secure salvation. In this case conformity to the Mosaic Law was demanded, but "merit" earned by adherence to any other legal pattern would have been just as damaging.

We need to keep that in mind to understand Paul's blanket criticism of "law works." Any deeds done to gain God's favor are worthless, yes, worse than worthless. They are damning because they separate people from their only hope, the merits of Christ that are received by faith.

Paul leaves no doubt that these two stand in direct opposition to each other. Works are *man's doing*. Faith is accepting what *God has done* in Christ. Paul's thesis throughout is that justification comes not by works but by faith alone. This thesis is bolstered and undergirded by four supporting points:

1. The Galatians' own experience (3:1-5);
2. Abraham's case (3:6-9);
3. The difference between law and gospel (3:10-14);
4. The promise given already to Abraham (3:15-18).

The Galatians' own experience

3 **You foolish Galatians! Who has bewitched you? Before your very eyes Jesus Christ was clearly portrayed as crucified. ²I would like to learn just one thing from you: Did you receive the Spirit by observing the law, or by believing what you heard? ³Are you so foolish? After beginning with the Spirit, are you now trying to attain your goal by human effort? ⁴Have you suffered so much for nothing—if it really was for nothing? ⁵Does God give you his Spirit and work miracles among you because you observe the law, or because you believe what you heard?**

Paul now turns to the Galatians and addresses them directly, calling them "foolish." The Greek word Paul uses here doesn't imply that they are ignorant or lacking in intellectual gifts. Rather, Paul's complaint is that they're not using the mental gifts and capabilities they do have. They really should know better!

The only explanation Paul can give himself for their folly is that they've been "bewitched." The use of this term does not imply that Paul really believed in sorcery and magic and that he assumed someone had put the Galatians under a spell. It is a mode of expression such as we might use with someone whose actions completely baffle us. We may blurt out, "What in the world has gotten into you?"

That's Paul's reaction when he sees what the Galatians have done with the message he preached so clearly to them. Paul preached Christ crucified. When Paul says that Christ was "clearly portrayed" as crucified, he's using a Greek term that actually conveys the idea of putting up a poster or a placard. When Paul was done preaching, the centrality of Christ's death on the cross was as clear as if someone had enlarged a picture of the scene at Calvary and mounted it on a billboard for all to see. There could be no mistaking that trust in the crucified Christ, and not in a person's own paltry works, was the heart of Paul's message.

With the centrality of Christ's sacrifice so graphically portrayed to them and after Paul had urged them to accept this Savior by faith, Paul now directs a searching question to them. "Tell me just this one thing," he demands. "Did you receive the Spirit by observing the law, or by believing what you heard?"

The full scope of Paul's question becomes even more apparent if in our translation we remove the article from before "law" to conform to the original. Literally Paul asks, "Was it by law-works that you received the Spirit or by hearing with faith?" His question is, "Did you have to *do* anything, or was it merely a matter of *receiving*, of trusting, of taking what God was giving you?"

Before taking up the answer to that question, let's look a bit more closely at what is being either earned or received as a gift. Paul asks, "Did you receive the Spirit by observing the law, or by believing what you heard?" How we understand this verse depends to some extent on what we determine to be the exact meaning of *pneuma*, the Greek word for "Spirit." The original does not indicate whether it should be taken as "Spirit" (capital *S*) or "spirit" (small *s*). With a capital *S* it refers to the Holy Spirit. With the lowercase *s* it refers to the spirit in man, his spiritual nature. For example, in chapter 5 Paul will speak of the battle in a Christian between the "flesh" and the "spirit." There he is referring to the antagonism between the believer's spiritual nature and his fleshly or carnal nature. Call it the "new man" fighting against the "old Adam." In this passage also it would work very nicely for Paul to be referring to that new spiritual life that the Galatians enjoyed as Christians.

However, we really have no problem with the NIV translators' choice of the capital *S*, thus referring to the Holy Spirit, for there can be no true spiritual life without the work of the Holy Spirit.

Whichever meaning we choose, the point of Paul's question is this: When you became Christians and entered into that blissful spiritual state that became yours as a consequence of my bringing you the gospel, did that happen because you did something or because you believed what you heard? The answer, of course, was obvious. They didn't work for their spiritual life. They didn't launch into a program of keeping certain rules (either the Mosaic Law or any other legal pattern of works). They simply believed. They took Paul's message at face value and rested their whole confidence in Christ's merit.

That being the case, Paul now confronts the Galatians with another question. "Are you so foolish? After beginning with the Spirit, are you now trying to attain your goal by human effort?" They began without legal observances or works and had in this way received the blessings of true spiritual life with God. What a classic example of changing horses midstream. How foolish it was for them now to switch over to works of law to complete their spiritual life— a life that began so well without works or legal observances!

Paul has spoken of the beginning and the end of their spiritual life. Now he directs attention to their present state. He inquires: "Have you suffered so much for nothing—if it really was for nothing? Does God give you his Spirit and work miracles among you because you observe the law, or because you believe what you heard?" Actually, the Greek verb used in this verse (translated "suffered") is neutral. Basically it means only "to experience." The things experienced can be good or bad. The context must indicate and determine the precise shading of the verb.

From the following verse, it seems that Paul is talking about good things that are being experienced, rather than evil things suffered. It seems preferable, therefore, to have Paul ask, "Have you experienced so many good things from God in vain?"

He then follows up with the good things that are still daily happening to them. He asks, "Does the One who continues to give you his Spirit and work miracles among you do that because you observe the law, or because you believe what you heard?" Note that Paul hasn't written off his beloved Galatians. To be sure, they are under pressure from the Judaizers whose arguments sound tempting. They may be undergoing temptation. They may even be leaning toward doing things that are foolish. But Paul gives them the benefit of the doubt. They are still children of God. God is still working in them. "How is it that all these things are happening among you?" Paul asks. They can fill in the answer themselves: Not by works, but only by God's grace in Christ that is accepted *by faith*.

Paul doesn't say it. He doesn't have to. Prudence and common sense would give the counsel: "Stay with a winner!"

Abraham's case

However, Paul's argument didn't rest only on the Galatians' own experience, in which they received God's gracious blessings by faith without working for any of them. He directs them to another example where it was clearly estab-

55

lished that God's greatest blessings were received by faith, the case of the patriarch Abraham.

⁶Consider Abraham: "He believed God, and it was credited to him as righteousness." ⁷Understand, then, that those who believe are children of Abraham. ⁸The Scripture foresaw that God would justify the Gentiles by faith, and announced the gospel in advance to Abraham: "All nations will be blessed through you." ⁹So those who have faith are blessed along with Abraham, the man of faith.

Abraham was properly revered as the father of the Jewish nation. When God chose Abraham and his family to be the bearers of the promise and the family from whom the Savior would be born, God was designating them as his chosen nation.

Kinship with Abraham was understandably a source of pride for loyal Jews. Unfortunately, it also became a source of misplaced confidence. When Jesus called his Jewish hearers to repentance and tried to show them their need for a savior, they objected, "We are Abraham's children." That connection with Abraham was their "ticket to heaven." When the Judaizers urged the Galatians to accept and observe the Mosaic Law, they touted the advantages of aligning themselves with the "chosen people" and in this way becoming "children of Abraham."

In response, Paul takes up the case of Abraham. He declares: Even Abraham did not enter into a right relationship with God by what he did. Rather, "he *believed* God, and it was credited to him as righteousness."

Abraham did not put his confidence in anything he himself did, but trusted in God. He put his confidence in what God had promised. The object of Abraham's trust and confidence was nothing other than God's promised Savior and

Messiah. Jesus bears clear testimony to Abraham's faith when he tells his Jewish opponents, "Your father Abraham rejoiced at the thought of seeing my day; he saw it and was glad" (John 8:56).

Note that the Bible doesn't say Abraham changed his pattern of living so as to become righteous enough for God to accept him on this basis. Rather, Abraham believed in Christ, the promised Savior, and that faith "was credited to him as righteousness." God looked at Abraham as if he were righteous. God credited him with a righteousness that was not the patriarch's own. God "justified" him by crediting, or imputing, to him the righteousness of Christ. And all this came to Abraham "by faith." By faith Abraham received everything God had promised him.

But someone may say: That's all well and good for Abraham. But what about others? What about the Galatians? What about us? Paul answers these questions by extending the case of Abraham to make it a general rule when he declares, "Understand, then, that those who believe are children of Abraham."

Entering into that blissful relationship of being accepted by God, being declared justified, is not something that depends upon birth or blood but is open to all who believe and trust in God's promised Savior. Because justification is by faith, it can include the Galatian believers and us and all believers in between.

In fact, from the very beginning—even when God was calling Abraham—he had in mind to save people by faith in Christ. Hence Paul can say, "The Scripture foresaw that God would justify the Gentiles by faith, and announced the gospel in advance to Abraham: 'All nations will be blessed through you.'"

To be sure, when he called Abraham, God made some great and precious promises to him. He promised to give Abraham a special land and make him into a great nation. These were not universal promises, though. Not everyone is born a Jew, nor are all privileged to live in the Promised Land of Palestine.

But God also said to Abraham, "*All nations* will be blessed through you." How can that be? Because the heart of God's promise to Abraham centered on the Savior who would be born from his line. For that reason Paul can say that in the promise of a Savior made to Abraham, God "announced the gospel in advance." God foresaw that the Gentiles also would be accepting the promised Savior by faith—and would be justified by that faith. Hence Paul can make this generalization: "So those who have faith are blessed along with Abraham, the man of faith."

Abraham was blessed by faith in Christ, just as everyone else who trusts in Christ. It is the gospel that saves, not the law with its demands of obedience and performance. In fact, not only does the law not save, but it puts people under its curse. Paul brings that thought into sharp focus in his next section.

The difference between law and gospel

[10]All who rely on observing the law are under a curse, for it is written: "Cursed is everyone who does not continue to do everything written in the Book of the Law." [11]Clearly no one is justified before God by the law, because, "The righteous will live by faith." [12]The law is not based on faith; on the contrary, "The man who does these things will live by them." [13]Christ redeemed us from the curse of the law by becoming a curse for us, for it is written: "Cursed is everyone who is hung on a tree." [14]He redeemed us in order that the blessing given to

Abraham might come to the Gentiles through Christ Jesus, so that by faith we might receive the promise of the Spirit.

The Judaizers were bothering the Galatians by insisting that they keep the Mosaic Law with its Old Testament rites and ceremonies. They do not seem to have denied that Jesus of Nazareth was the Messiah, the promised Savior. What they questioned was Paul's teaching that faith in Christ alone could save people.

They insisted that something more was necessary: becoming proselytes to Judaism—accepting the precepts of the Mosaic Law, such as observing the dietary laws, keeping the Sabbath, accepting the rite of circumcision—in short, *doing* something to be sure of God's favor.

Paul counters: That course of action is dangerous—yes, even fatal—for the law itself makes a most dreadful threat to those who keep it imperfectly. The apostle quotes Deuteronomy 27:26: "Cursed is everyone who does not continue to do everything written in the Book of the Law." Note that there are three ironclad demands in the Deuteronomy passage. The law demands *continuous, flawless performance.*

Let's examine these three—in reverse order. *Performance.* By definition, a law tells us what we are to *do.* It demands performance. *Flawless.* Nonperformance leads to punishment. But not just any kind of performance is acceptable. It has to be perfect and complete. Note the Deuteronomy passage's demand for performance of "*everything* written in the Book of the Law." God declares, "Be holy because I, the LORD your God, am holy" (Leviticus 19:2). Catching that point, James says in his epistle, "Whoever keeps the whole law and yet stumbles at just one point is guilty of breaking all of it" (2:10). *Continual.* James 2:10 also illustrates this third element. We dare not keep all the law only some of the time.

No, as Paul points out through the Deuteronomy quotation, we must continue to do everything written in God's law.

That threefold demand makes sinners of us all and puts us under the law's curse. The Judaizers' way doesn't work. But, fortunately, Scripture doesn't hold us to the Judaizers' plan of salvation. It points us to something quite different. Paul continues: "Clearly no one is justified before God by the law, because, 'The righteous will live by faith.' The law is not based on faith; on the contrary, 'The man who does these things will live by them.'"

God's plan of salvation is not based on human performance but on faith. We have just been directed to the example of Abraham. He *believed*, and that faith was credited to him as righteousness. Now Paul adds the testimony of the prophet Habakkuk who, speaking by inspiration, said, "The righteous will live by faith" (Habakkuk 2:4). *Faith* is what God looks for—and the law with its demands for performance has nothing to do with faith.

Take an illustration from everyday life. I may be totally convinced of the value of a 55-miles-per-hour speed limit on our highways. It conserves fuel; it reduces the number of accidents; it saves lives. I may agree with that law. I may have complete "faith" in its value. But I can't say I have always obeyed it perfectly, and I'll still be ticketed if I drive 70 miles per hour. *Faith* and *performance* stand worlds apart.

Returning to the sinner's hope for salvation, God says, "The righteous will live by faith." That can't include the law because, as Paul indicates, "The law is not based on faith; on the contrary, 'The man who *does* these things will live by them.'"

We can't be saved by our "doing." Our disobedience, our nonperformance, leaves the law no choice but to condemn us and put us under its curse. But, thank God, there is an escape from its just punishment. "Christ redeemed us from the curse of the law by becoming a curse for us, for it is written: 'Cursed is everyone who is hung on a tree.'" Here again Paul is quoting from Deuteronomy, which establishes that Christ in his crucifixion did indeed become a curse, for "cursed is everyone who is hung on a tree" (Deuteronomy 21:23). But the grand truth that Paul here wishes to emphasize is *why* Jesus became a curse. He did it for us, to redeem us from the curse of the law.

To "redeem" means to "buy back," to pay the price necessary to set a slave free. Christ paid what we owed. He took our place. He did what we could not do. He settled our account with the law. By his perfect life and innocent death on the cross Christ made a historical reality of what Abraham and "all nations" had received only by promise. As Paul puts it, "He redeemed us in order that the blessing given to Abraham might come to the Gentiles through Christ Jesus."

And how does this priceless blessing come to the Galatians, to us, and to all believers? Paul continues, "So that *by faith* we might receive the promise of the Spirit." The law demands performance, and that we cannot supply. Consequently, that way leads to a curse. The only alternative is to despair of our own works and turn in faith to Christ's merits. Therein lies peace, security, and salvation.

The promise given already to Abraham

Paul has indicated that there is a vast difference between law and gospel. The law requires and makes demands. It *takes*; it looks for obedience. The gospel, on the other hand, *gives*; it bestows gifts on those who have no claim to them or reason to expect them.

61

But there is yet another difference that's useful for Paul's readers to keep in mind: the matter of timing. God's gospel promise actually was given before the Mosaic ceremonies.

Good teacher that he is, Paul helps his readers see the significance of that difference in timing by giving us an example to illustrate the point. He compares the difference in timing to what happens in the matter of administering a person's last will and testament or "covenant" as it's called in the NIV translation.

15Brothers, let me take an example from everyday life. Just as no one can set aside or add to a human covenant that has been duly established, so it is in this case. 16The promises were spoken to Abraham and to his seed. The Scripture does not say "and to seeds," meaning many people, but "and to your seed," meaning one person, who is Christ. 17What I mean is this: The law, introduced 430 years later, does not set aside the covenant previously established by God and thus do away with the promise. 18For if the inheritance depends on the law, then it no longer depends on a promise; but God in his grace gave it to Abraham through a promise.

Paul invites us to think of how a will works, particularly in two aspects. First, a will by definition is a formal document in which the maker expresses his final wishes and desires. He states how he wants to distribute things of value to his heirs. A will is essentially a *promise* to give property or goods.

A second thing to note is the *binding nature* of a properly made will or covenant. The maker of the will can change things as much as he wants, but if it has been duly established and the maker of the will dies, then others can't arbitrarily change the stipulations of the will to suit their own fancy. These two features of a will or covenant have significance in the important doctrinal matter that Paul wishes to illustrate.

First, God's covenant with Abraham was a promise. Paul writes: "The promises were spoken to Abraham and to his seed. The Scripture does not say 'and to seeds,' meaning many people, but 'and to your seed,' meaning one person, who is Christ."

The apostle points out that the heart and core of God's covenant with Abraham was the promise of a Savior. To be sure, there was the promise that Abraham would become a great nation and a special land would be given to him, but that was not a universal promise to all people. That was spoken specifically to the Israelites living in the Promised Land of Canaan.

But Abraham was also told, "Through your offspring [literally, "Seed"] all nations on earth will be blessed" (Genesis 22:18; see also 26:4; 28:14). The fulfillment of that promise rested not on his many descendants ("seeds") but on one "Seed," Christ.

Having established that the promise to Abraham was essentially a messianic promise, Paul comes to the second of his two points of comparison with a will or covenant. The covenant with Abraham was duly established through God's repeated promise of a Savior for Abraham and all the nations of the earth. And like a human will or covenant, God's covenant with Abraham cannot be changed.

We recall that after Abraham died, the patriarchal family moved to Egypt and stayed there for roughly the next four centuries. Here they grew to be a great nation, as promised, but they also fell into bondage to the Egyptians until they were freed by God under Moses' leadership. After they were delivered, they journeyed to Mount Sinai, where God gave them the law code generally referred to as the Mosaic Law. It was the ceremonies and rituals of this law that the Judaizers were urging the Galatians to keep, as an addition to the simple trust in the gospel promise Paul had proclaimed.

Paul points out that the Judaizers were misapplying the Mosaic Law and acting like dishonest heirs who tamper with the conditions of a will, in their case God's original covenant with Abraham. Paul counters, "The law, introduced 430 years later, does not set aside the covenant previously established by God and thus do away with the promise." Paul's point is: We don't ride roughshod over a human will. How much less ought the Judaizers be allowed to overturn God's covenant with Abraham with a document that didn't come into being until 430 years later.

Along these same lines, Paul raises another objection to the Judaizers' way of doing things, namely, that they were changing the whole nature of how God dealt with his people under the Abrahamic covenant.

We've noted that a will is a person's formal promise to *give* property or goods to his heirs. It's a gift to them, not something they still need to earn or buy. Paul rightly asserts, "If the inheritance depends on the law [doing some required thing], then it no longer depends on a promise [receiving it freely as a gift]."

If the executor of a will told an heir, "You've been named as the recipient of your uncle's farm, but you'll have to pay a thousand dollars an acre to get it or work ten years for it," the heir would cry foul, and rightly so. Paul makes it clear that the same holds true in the spiritual realm. He says, "God in his grace gave it [the inheritance of salvation] to Abraham through a promise." Paul was right in preaching to the Galatians a message of salvation purely by grace, a free gift from God, because that's how God gave it to Abraham. The Judaizers messed it up by suggesting that in addition to believing in Christ, certain ceremonies had to be kept and some rituals needed to be observed if one was to be sure of salvation. It's a common mistake, one still made by Christian religious leaders who advocate faith in Christ but then require works of penance, urge the performance of certain tasks, or look for monetary contributions at a prescribed level or for any other required "law-work." Relying on our performance nullifies God's grace. Law and gospel don't mix.

Christians are free from the law

Using the everyday example of how the inheritance system works, Paul has illustrated that God's plan of salvation, "duly established" in his covenant with Abraham, rests on God's "promise" and is not dependent in any way on man's performance. It is a gospel covenant, not a law arrangement. So well does the inheritance picture serve to show the superiority of gift and grace over law and performance that Paul anticipates someone may wonder about the value of the law. Paul addresses that point next.

A description of the law

Paul begins his description of the law by listing four of its weaknesses.

¹⁹**What, then, was the purpose of the law? It was added because of transgressions until the Seed to whom the promise referred had come. The law was put into effect through angels by a mediator. ²⁰A mediator, however, does not represent just one party; but God is one.**
²¹**Is the law, therefore, opposed to the promises of God? Absolutely not! For if a law had been given that could impart life, then righteousness would certainly have come by the law. ²²But the Scripture declares that the whole world is a prisoner of sin, so that what was promised, being given through faith in Jesus Christ, might be given to those who believe.**

²³**Before this faith came, we were held prisoners by the law, locked up until faith should be revealed. ²⁴So the law was put in charge to lead us to Christ that we might be justified by faith. ²⁵Now that faith has come, we are no longer under the supervision of the law.**

The inherent weakness of the Mosaic Law shows itself in four ways, and these are all enumerated in the first paragraph quoted (verses 19,20). The second paragraph quoted (verses 21,22) forms a commentary on the second weakness, while the third paragraph quoted (verses 23-25) addresses primarily the third weakness. The four weaknesses that Paul identifies are

1. The Mosaic Law was not primary, but was "added" to something superior, something already in existence.
2. The law had to do with sin and "transgressions," not salvation.
3. The law was of limited duration, "until the Seed . . . had come."
4. The law required a "mediator."

The law was "added." The Judaizers were minded to attach undue weight and importance to the keeping of the Mosaic ceremonies and rituals, such as observing festivals and dietary regulations, as though these were the important things God expected from his people. Paul is defending his message of salvation by faith alone in Christ Jesus without the addition of any human performance, including the keeping of Mosaic regulations, which didn't come on the scene until 430 years after God had promised a Savior to Abraham. Not the Mosaic Law but the promise made to Abraham was central in God's dealing with his chosen people. Even for the

Jews, the law was added later and was always of a secondary nature, serving in a supporting role.

"Because of transgressions." Furthermore, Paul says that the law was added "because of transgressions." As the Israelites showed repeatedly in their 40 years in the wilderness, they were a stubborn and stiff-necked people. They needed training. The regulations set down by God at Mount Sinai and agreed to by the Israelites served admirably for this training and correcting process.

To be sure, the special instructions given to Israel in order to control their worship life and the laws regarding clean and unclean foods that controlled their eating patterns served to separate them from the pagan world. Thus these regulations hedged them about and protected them as God's special people.

Most importantly, these regulations were a constant reminder of how things stood between the Israelites and their God. Every breaking of the law, every neglect of the many individual precepts was a testimony to the thoroughgoing sinfulness that marred their relationship to a just and holy God. God's law showed Israel its sin! And God clearly stated, "The soul who sins is the one who will die." Every bloody sacrifice was a visible reminder that the wages of sin is death and that sinners can be spared only by having a substitute take their place and suffer death for them.

The law could teach the need for righteousness, but it could not give the required righteousness. Therein lay a serious limitation. The law could not provide salvation as the Judaizers claimed; it could only point to and prepare for the salvation that needed to come from another source, namely, the promised Savior. Speaking of the law's weakness of being only secondary and supporting, Paul asks: "Is the law, therefore, opposed to the promises of God? Absolutely not!

For if a law had been given that could impart life, then righteousness would certainly have come by the law. But the Scripture declares that the whole world is a prisoner of sin, so that what was promised, being given through faith in Jesus Christ, might be given to those who believe."

"Until the Seed had come." A third weakness of the Mosaic Law was that it was intended by God to be of limited duration. Paul tells the Galatians that the law was added because of transgressions "until the Seed to whom the promise referred had come."

The Old Testament, with its many specific rules and regulations, was a time of preparation for the New Testament age marked by the Christian liberty that comes through faith in Christ Jesus. It is the New Testament "faith" in the Savior who has come in fulfillment of God's promise to Abraham that Paul is speaking of. He explains, "Before this faith came, we were held prisoners by the law, locked up until faith should be revealed. So the law was put in charge to lead us to Christ that we might be justified by faith. Now that faith has come, we are no longer under the supervision of the law."

Much of this section continues the idea of the secondary and supportive, even supervisory, role of the law. Israel is pictured as a prisoner locked up under the law. Surely the Judaizers gave bad news and offered bad advice when they urged a continuation of the law's control.

Paul paints a brighter picture. "All those restrictions and limitations have outlived their usefulness and have been done away with," Paul tells the Galatians. To see that a bit more clearly we should perhaps take a closer look at verse 24. Some readers will no doubt remember how the King James Version rendered this verse: "The law was our schoolmaster to bring us unto Christ." Our quotation from the NIV reflects the same questionable idea. It reads, "So the law was put in charge to lead us to Christ." Actually, the law isn't our "teacher" in that it "brings us to Christ." Only the gospel can do that. A footnote in the NIV suggests this translation: "The law was put in charge until Christ came." That translation takes into account Paul's point that the law has limited duration.

The original Greek says that the law was our *paidagogos*. A paidagogos was the slave who accompanied a schoolboy to make sure that he didn't get into trouble on the way to school and that he actually got there. The instructing itself was done by others. So Paul is saying, "The law served merely as a chaperon—and that only until God fulfilled his gospel promise and sent his Son." "Before this faith came, we were held prisoners by the law. . . . Now that faith has come, we are no longer under the supervision of the law." Again, the Judaizers were wrong in insisting that the Mosaic Law was still valid.

The law required a "mediator." Finally, Paul saw the law's requirement of a mediator as a weakness. He states: "The law was put into effect through angels by a mediator. A mediator, however, does not represent just one party; but God is one."

A number of interpretations have been suggested for this passage, the diversity being caused partly by the fact that we're not told much in Scripture about the role of angels in putting the law into effect. But the role of the angels isn't Paul's major point. His interest centers more on the mediator.

The Mosaic Law given on Mount Sinai was a two-sided (bilateral) covenant in that it involved two parties and had conditions attached to it. God told Israel, If you will do thus and so, then I will bless you in this and that way. Because the covenant involved agreement between two parties, the arrangement needed a go-between, a mediator to secure assurance of agreement by both sides. But that agreement

69

immediately becomes tentative and insecure when we realize that one of the agreeing parties was fickle and unreliable Israel, the headstrong and stubborn people who needed to be chaperoned, guided, and corrected.

How infinitely better and more secure to have just one party making a one-sided agreement, particularly when the maker of the promise is the absolutely faithful and reliable God of heaven and earth. And that was the case with the gospel promise made to Abraham. Without any conditions or stipulations, God in his grace simply announced to him, "I will make of you a great nation; I will give you a special land to inhabit; I will bless all nations of the earth in the Savior who will be born from your line." The Mosaic Law, hampered by the need for participation and obedience on man's part, can't hold a candle to God's gospel promise.

The gospel promise—made by God to Abraham, fulfilled in Christ, proclaimed by Paul—is a sure and reliable basis for confidence for all believers, who by definition are people not doing anything on their own but simply receiving God's grace.

26You are all sons of God through faith in Christ Jesus, 27for all of you who were baptized into Christ have clothed yourselves with Christ. 28There is neither Jew nor Greek, slave nor free, male nor female, for you are all one in Christ Jesus. 29If you belong to Christ, then you are Abraham's seed, and heirs according to the promise.

"If you belong to Christ," if you know Jesus as your Savior by faith worked in you by your baptism and the other means of grace, "then you are Abraham's seed." Faith in Christ makes the righteousness that Christ earned for us our own. It "clothes" us with Christ, so that God sees not our filthy sins and shortcomings but only Christ's merits and his perfect righteousness earned for us on the cross. Performance and merit earned by our keeping any legal pattern do not count before God. Note the repetition of the inclusive "all" in these verses. With him all believers in Christ stand on the same plane, regardless of whether they are Jews or Greeks, slaves or free, male or female. All believers are in line for a full share of the inheritance.

The parable of the minor heir,
an illustration from everyday life

The picture of heirs and their inheritance suggests for Paul another way of looking at the believer's relationship to the law. He states:

4 **What I am saying is that as long as the heir is a child, he is no different from a slave, although he owns the whole estate. ²He is subject to guardians and trustees until the time set by his father. ³So also, when we were children, we were in slavery under the basic principles of the world. ⁴But when the time had fully come, God sent his Son, born of a woman, born under law, ⁵to redeem those under law, that we might receive the full rights of sons. ⁶Because you are sons, God sent the Spirit of his Son into our hearts, the Spirit who calls out, "Abba, Father." ⁷So you are no longer a slave, but a son; and since you are a son, God has made you also an heir.**

Our minds are constructed by the Creator in such a way that we learn better from having one thing compared to another. In order to understand something unknown or unfamiliar, it helps us to have it compared with something more familiar and better known to us. For example, to give us a picture of how nervous someone was before having to get up and give an important speech, a person might say of him, He was pacing back and forth *like a caged lion*.

Comparisons using "like" or "as" are technically called "similes." If you extend a simile by adding a few more details and making a little descriptive story out of it, you get a parable. Jesus often taught in parables ("the kingdom of heaven is like"), and Paul here uses a parable to teach a bit more fully the relationship of Old Testament Jewish believers to the Mosaic Law.

His illustration is taken from something in everyday life, namely, the matter of wills and inheritance. Paul explains, "What I am saying is that as long as the heir is a child, he is no different from a slave, although he owns the whole estate. He is subject to guardians and trustees until the time set by his father" (verses 1,2).

A millionaire's son may in fact be the owner of everything that his father possesses, but the wise father is not going to turn everything over to his son until he's capable of managing things properly. The minor son first needs to go through a period of training and disciplining in which he does not look much different from a slave or an ordinary household servant. Uncomfortable as it may be, that period of training, limited to the time frame set by the father, is of great value for the prospective heir.

Now comes the parable's point of comparison. Paul relates this everyday scene of the minor heir under the guardianship of a household servant to the Old Testament Jews in their relationship to the Mosaic law. He explains, "So also, when we were children, we were in slavery under the basic principles of the world. But when the time had fully come, God sent his Son . . . that we might receive the full rights of sons" (verses 3-5).

The heir's receiving the "full rights of sons" is not something brought about or effected by the temporary training period. Receiving the inheritance rests solely and completely on the father's activity of fulfilling his promise. So too, the Mosaic Law was not the vehicle through which God brought about his great blessing of salvation; that came, rather, in God the Father's good time, through the fulfillment of the promise of a Savior for all nations, given much earlier to Abraham.

Note how completely Paul describes God's saving activity: "But when the time had fully come, God sent his Son, born of a woman, born under law, to redeem those under law, that we might receive the full rights of sons."

"God sent his Son"—the Savior of the world was none other than true God. God's son was "born of a woman"—the Savior of the world deigned to be born of a virgin and become also true man. He was "born under law, to redeem those under law"—though he was true God, the Giver of the law, yet willingly as true man he put himself "under law" that he might keep it for "those under law" and thus earn for them the righteousness that a just and holy God properly expects and demands.

It is important to note that in these verses the term "law" does not have the article *the* either time it is used, as though it were limited just to the Mosaic Law that has been under discussion. It's broader than that. "Law" here refers to everything that God rightly demands of all people. The Savior's work was not restricted to serving just his Jewish countrymen. It included the "all nations" envisioned in the promise given to Abraham and hence included also the Galatians. That is why we must not restrict Paul's use of "we" to himself and other Jews when he now goes on to state that the purpose of God's sending his Son as Savior was "that *we* might receive the full rights of sons." The pronoun "we" is an inclusive term.

Paul includes the Galatians when he here speaks of the blessings of full sonship. This becomes evident in the next two verses. Paul addresses the Galatians directly in the second person, saying, "Because *you* are sons, God sent the Spirit of his Son into our hearts, the Spirit who calls out, '*Abba*, Father.'"

Continuing to address the Galatians directly in the second person, Paul even switches to the singular pronoun to assure each and every Galatian individually of the blessings brought by the Savior sent at God's good time. He gives them this assurance: "So you are no longer a slave, but a son; and since you are a son, God has made you also an heir." In Christ the Galatians, as dear children talking to *Abba*, their dear Father, can confidently address God as sons and heirs who are sure of their inheritance, an eternal place with God in heaven.

We have heard much about the Jewish nation and their rather uncomfortable confinement under the Mosaic Law. As non-Jews, the Gentile Galatians never were under these specific regulations. But they too had been freed from a tremendous burden of legal requirements—in their case, one imposed by their own former false ideas of how they needed to serve their pagan idols and "non-gods." The apostle reminds them:

8Formerly, when you did not know God, you were slaves to those who by nature are not gods. 9But now that you know God—or rather are known by God—how is it that you are turning back to those weak and miserable principles? Do you wish to be enslaved by them all over again? 10You are observing special days and months and seasons and years! 11I fear for you, that somehow I have wasted my efforts on you.

There really are only two plans of salvation in the world: merit or grace. People by nature are always inclined to work with the merit system. They reason: I need to do this and that to satisfy my god. If I do enough, I'll be acceptable to him

74

and thus receive blessing from him. The alternative is grace: receiving God's blessings totally as a gift, purely out of his goodness and love, without any merit on the recipient's part.

The Galatians, with their naturalistic, pagan religious background, came from a situation in which they had been "slaves to those who by nature are not gods." With endless ritual and sacrifice and personal piety they had tried to satisfy their heathen idols.

But through Paul's preachment of a gospel of pure grace, God had rescued them from this slavery. Actually, the Galatians didn't come to God; God came to them so that they have now become "known by God." They have been declared sons and heirs of every gift and blessing through faith in the Savior whom God has sent. The Galatians did nothing; they received everything as a pure gift of God's grace.

Now, however, after having come to know the glorious freedom of receiving everything as a free gift through the grace system of salvation, the Galatians were flirting with the idea of going back to the merit system. Almost unable to comprehend such folly, Paul blurts out: "How is it that you are turning back to those weak and miserable principles? Do you wish to be enslaved by them all over again?"

To be sure, the Galatians weren't considering reverting to their former heathen religious practices, but they were doing something that in principle was just as bad. In place of their former pagan ways of trying to earn favor by doing things for their heathen gods, they were trying to please the God of grace who has done everything for them. They were thinking of following the suggestion of the Judaizers, who said, "To be sure of your salvation, you must keep the Mosaic regulations." As Paul points out, this is just a variation of the old merit plan.

That we are right in seeing the threat as coming from Judaizers is evident from the charge Paul now makes: "You are observing special days and months and seasons and years!" The reference is to the Mosaic regulations governing the weekly Sabbath, the new moon and monthly festivals, and the annual festivals. The specific observances the Galatians were following may be different from what they did for their former heathen idols, but the principle of trying by their performance to please God was shockingly the same. The Galatians were on the verge of trading in everything that had been given to them as a free gift of God's grace in Christ and were trying to earn it by their own performance—in this case, by keeping the Mosaic ceremonies. Understandably Paul fumes: "What you're doing is dumb; you're shooting yourself in the foot! I fear for you, that somehow I have wasted my efforts on you."

Free from the law:
the example of the Galatians' own conversion

The letter to the Galatians is an example of rapid and wide mood swings. Recall that this section of the letter opened with the almost angry question "You foolish Galatians! Who has bewitched you?" (3:1). The apostle then proceeded to a calm and reasoned appeal to their own experience of receiving God's blessings by faith, just as Abraham did (3:2-9).

We have just heard Paul allow himself what might fairly be called an emotional outburst: "I'm afraid I've wasted my time on you!" In the interest of winning over the Galatians and bringing them to their senses, Paul immediately shifts to an entirely different tone. He calls them "brothers," and in his warmest and most winsome voice pleads with them and urges them to think back on how good things were for them when they first accepted his message of pure grace without the addition of any works.

¹²I plead with you, brothers, become like me, for I became like you. You have done me no wrong. ¹³As you know, it was because of an illness that I first preached the gospel to you. ¹⁴Even though my illness was a trial to you, you did not treat me with contempt or scorn. Instead, you welcomed me as if I were an angel of God, as if I were Christ Jesus himself. ¹⁵What has happened to all your joy? I can testify that, if you could have done so, you would have torn out your eyes and given them to me. ¹⁶Have I now become your enemy by telling you the truth?

Paul reminds the Galatians of the circumstances surrounding his first visit to them. He tells them, "As you know, it was because of an illness that I first preached the gospel to you." The Galatians knew all about that first visit—but we don't. In the absence of solid information, a number of theories regarding Paul's "illness" have been advanced. Because of the very short time spent in the coastal lowland region of Perga on Paul's first missionary journey and his immediate departure to the higher, interior parts of Asia Minor (that is, Galatia), some have supposed that Paul suffered from malaria. On the strength of Paul's remark that the Galatians would have been willing to tear their eyes out and give them to Paul, others have concluded that Paul may have had eye problems. In 2 Corinthians 12:7 Paul speaks of some disability, "a thorn in [the] flesh," that hampered him. Perhaps that is what he is referring to here. We just don't have that information.

Paul seems to imply that his disability made him unattractive and disgusting somehow and could have put people off. He was a "trial" to them, but they did not treat him with scorn or contempt. Instead, so overjoyed were they at the liberating message of God's free grace in Christ, which gave them forgiveness of sins, peace with God, and the assurance of an open heaven, that they welcomed Paul as if he were "an angel of God."

Sadly Paul now asks, "What has happened to your all joy?" We know the answer, of course. Their joy in the liberating message of the gospel had been spoiled by the arrival of the Judaizers, who insisted that in addition to believing in Christ, the Galatians needed also to obey the Old Testament ceremonies.

The Judaizers had spoiled the message and slandered the messenger by saying that Paul was only a Johnny-come-lately, not a real apostle at all, and not in sync with what Christ's true apostles were teaching and what God's people in Jerusalem believed.

Confused in their minds and unsettled by the thought that they may have been duped by Paul, the Galatians' initial joy in the gospel evaporated. Add to this the fact that Paul has had to say some rather sharp things to them in this letter, and we are not surprised at Paul's question: "Have I now become your enemy by telling you the truth?"

Again, the answer is obvious. Is it a loveless act to take a sharp knife away from a toddler? Is the park ranger doing us a disservice by warning us back from a steep cliff? Was it wrong for Paul to alert the Galatians to the danger of listening to the faith-destroying error of people who were interested in themselves rather than in the Galatians and their welfare?

Paul considers it a "given" that defending the truth and exposing error and perversity have not made him an enemy to the Galatians. So he resumes his sharp and direct criticism of error and the Judaistic errorists, a criticism that at the same time reflects his loving concern for the Galatians and their spiritual welfare.

¹⁷**Those people are zealous to win you over, but for no good. What they want is to alienate you from us, so that you may be zealous for them. ¹⁸It is fine to be zealous, provided the purpose is good, and to be so always and not just when I am with you. ¹⁹My dear children, for whom I am again in the pains of childbirth until Christ is formed in you, ²⁰how I wish I could be with you now and change my tone, because I am perplexed about you!**

The term "zealous" is a key concept in this part of Paul's presentation to the Galatians. "Those people," the Judaizers, were zealous to win the Galatians over, but they were not doing it from a proper motive. They were not trying to be helpful to the Galatians; they were operating with totally self-serving motives. "What they want," Paul says, "is to alienate you [the Galatians] from us [Paul and his gospel coworkers], so that you may be zealous for them [the Judaizers]."

We need to remember that there was a difference between the "Judaizers" and the majority of the Jewish nation, who tenaciously held to the Old Testament because they didn't accept Jesus of Nazareth as the promised Messiah. The Judaizers were Christian in that they accepted Christ—but they insisted that wasn't enough. In addition to believing in Christ, they taught that a person also had to accept the Old Testament ceremonies in general and circumcision in particular. In other words, one had to get into God's good graces by going through Judaism; one had to become a "proselyte." By thus maintaining a form of Judaism, the Judaizers hoped to avoid persecution from the orthodox Jews. In his summary at the end of the letter, Paul touches on that dishonorable motive of the Judaizers a bit more directly. He charges: "Those who want to make a good impression outwardly are trying to compel you to be circumcised. The only reason they do this is to avoid being persecuted for the cross of Christ. . . .

They want you to be circumcised that they may boast about your flesh" (6:12,13).

Paul takes pains to point out that he is not jealous of the attention the Galatians were getting from the Judaizers. He explains the exact reason for his concerns. "It is fine to be zealous," he says—or as the original Greek could also be translated, "It's fine to be zealously sought—provided the purpose is good." Paul's complaint is not that the Galatians were zealous or that they were being zealously sought. That would be fine as long as the cause was a good one. But that was not the case here! The Judaizers' zeal was selfish. They hoped to get ahead by being able to say they had won the Galatians away from Paul and converted them to their cause.

The thought of losing the Galatians, and on such shabby grounds, was breaking Paul's heart—or, to use his picture, it was giving him pain as sharp as the labor pains of a woman in childbirth. He tells them, "My dear children, for whom I am again in the pains of childbirth until Christ is formed in you, how I wish I could be with you now and change my tone, because I am perplexed about you!"

It was stated earlier that this letter seems to have been written from Corinth on Paul's second missionary journey, while he was fully occupied in trying to start a mission congregation in that important Greek city. Paul couldn't drop everything and hurry back to Galatia, so he resorts to a letter. But it's a poor substitute. "If only I could be with you, and we could talk face to face," Paul laments. "Then I would be able to assess your spiritual condition, and I could adjust the tone and intensity of my voice accordingly."

Paul hadn't given up on the Galatians, and he certainly didn't want to think the worst about them, but their willingness to place themselves under the law once more after they had experienced God's grace was thoroughly perplexing to

Paul. Perhaps they didn't fully realize the implications of accepting the law as a means of salvation, so he asks, "Tell me, you who want to be under the law, are you not aware of what the law says?" (verse 21). And to help them see the full implication of the Judaizers' legalism, he utilized another figure of speech, an allegory.

The example of Ishmael and Isaac (an allegory)

In connection with the discussion of the minor heir (4:1-11) we spoke of how it helps the learning process to illustrate something that is unfamiliar by comparing it with something that is familiar and well-known. Such a comparison (simile) expanded into a descriptive little narrative is called a parable. A parable takes a common, everyday incident or occurrence that presents a general truth, puts "generic" people into it, and uses it to illustrate ("is like") a spiritual truth the teacher wants to explain.

In the section of the letter presently under discussion, Paul resorts to a slightly different way of making a comparison between two things that illustrate a spiritual truth. The figure of speech employed here is called an "allegory." Instead of taking a generic or general incident, Paul calls attention to a specific historical incident involving Abraham's slave girl Hagar and his wife, Sarah. The actions of these real people in a real situation are an example or illustration of the spiritual principle under discussion.

But not only does the original incident illustrate the point under consideration—in this case the relationship of law and gospel, human performance and merit versus God's gift and promise—it allows a broader application. It "says something else," which is literally what *allegory* means. The same wrong principle of trying to accomplish something by human performance that caused the problem in the Hagar and Ish-

81

mael incident is also at work in the wrong approach being advocated by the Judaizers.

In both cases there is only one prudent thing to do. "Get rid of the slave woman [Hagar] and her son [Ishmael]" translates into this advice: "Avoid the Judaizers and their followers."

As we read Paul's allegory, let us keep in mind the lead-in question that the allegory is to illustrate and answer: "Tell me, you who want to be under the law, are you not aware of what the law says?" Note the three components of Paul's allegorical answer:

1. The historical incident involving Abraham's slave girl Hagar and his wife, Sarah (verses 22,23);
2. The figurative counterpart—the two women signify two covenants: Hagar and Ishmael are the Judaizers, enslaved to the law; Sarah and Isaac are the Christian church, enjoying the freedom that comes with the gospel (verses 24-27);
3. The lesson to be learned and the application to be made—distance yourself from a dependence on law and a reliance on human achievement; cherish your gospel freedom (verses 28-31).

[21]Tell me, you who want to be under the law, are you not aware of what the law says? [22]For it is written that Abraham had two sons, one by the slave woman and the other by the free woman. [23]His son by the slave woman was born in the ordinary way; but his son by the free woman was born as the result of a promise.

God called Abraham at age 75 and promised that he would make of Abraham a great nation. Ten years later Abraham and Sarah still had no family. In desperation they devised the plan that Abraham should take their slave girl Hagar and have children by her. The result was the birth of Ishmael, as recounted in Genesis 16. It was an ill-advised plan that attempted to help God fulfill his promise by adding a human contribution to the divine plan.

But God's promise was that he would raise up a great nation from Abraham and Sarah. To make crystal clear that this family was the result of God's promise and did not come into being because of any human contribution, God delayed the blessed event of Isaac's birth for another 14 years, until a time when "his [Abraham's] body was as good as dead—since he was about a hundred years old—and . . . Sarah's womb was also dead" (Romans 4:19; see also Genesis 17:15,16).

Ishmael was inseparably linked with human performance. Isaac, on the other hand, was purely the result of God's promise, and he became the father of God's chosen people Israel.

The contrast between Ishmael and Isaac is in itself proof of the superiority of people trusting God's promise rather than trying to make things happen by their own contribution and accomplishments. But, as Paul tells us, this incident in the history of God's people is an allegory. The account has "another meaning." It "says something else." Or as the NIV translates:

²⁴These things may be taken figuratively, for the women represent two covenants. One covenant is from Mount Sinai and bears children who are to be slaves: This is Hagar. ²⁵Now Hagar stands for Mount Sinai in Arabia and corresponds to the present city of Jerusalem, because she is in slavery with her children. ²⁶But the Jerusalem that is above is free, and she is our mother. ²⁷For it is written:

> **"Be glad, O barren woman,**
> **who bears no children;**
> **break forth and cry aloud,**
> **you who have no labor pains;**

**because more are the children of the desolate woman
than of her who has a husband."**

Hagar, involved in an attempt to help make God's plan succeed, finds a parallel in the activity of the Judaizers. These people, largely inhabitants of Jerusalem, have ranged out as far as Galatia. Taking their motivation from Mount Sinai, that is, from the Mosaic Law given on Sinai, they teach people that in addition to believing in Christ they must also keep the Old Testament rules and regulations. In this way they were putting people into bondage under the Mosaic Law. Like the slave girl Hagar who bore slave children, so Judaizing Jerusalem "is in slavery with her children."

"But the Jerusalem that is above is free," Paul tells the Galatians, "and she is our mother." In contrast to the earthly Jerusalem, Paul directs the eyes of his readers to "the Jerusalem that is above." That Jerusalem is the assembly of all who believe in God's promise of a Savior. It's the Christian church—brought to faith by the gospel in Word and sacrament, sustained in that faith during its pilgrimage here on earth, and eventually gathered around the throne of the Lamb to thank and praise him eternally for the free gift of salvation.

Resting on God's grace alone, that Jerusalem does not require the keeping of any rules and regulations. She is truly "free" in that she makes no demands on her inhabitants but gives everything as a gift. And of that Jerusalem above Paul says, "She is our mother."

Relying simply on God's gospel promises might seem to be a slow and ineffective way to build the church. Hence we may be tempted to try and make the church more "efficient" by enlisting human help and participation. But that is mistaken and misplaced zeal. The tiny mustard seed will grow into a tree, as Jesus indicated in his parable. Or to stay with

Paul's picture, the Jerusalem above will be the mother of a large family, as foretold already in Isaiah 54:1: "Sing, O barren woman, you who never bore a child; burst into song, shout for joy, you who were never in labor; because more are the children of the desolate woman than of her who has a husband."

Paul's allegory sets two vastly different cases side by side: Ishmael, born of the slave woman as the result of human planning and conniving; Isaac, the son of the free woman, born under circumstances that made it unmistakably clear that only God's power and promise could have brought this miracle baby to a hundred-year-old father and a ninety-year-old mother.

As there was tension between these two quite different families in Abraham's life, so there is bound to be tension also between the adherents of the two covenants this allegory figuratively represents. Paul tells the Galatians:

28Now you, brothers, like Isaac, are children of promise. 29At that time the son born in the ordinary way persecuted the son born by the power of the Spirit. It is the same now. 30But what does the Scripture say? "Get rid of the slave woman and her son, for the slave woman's son will never share in the inheritance with the free woman's son." 31Therefore, brothers, we are not children of the slave woman, but of the free woman.

Genesis 21:9 tells us that Ishmael, "the son born in the ordinary way," bullied and teased his younger half-brother Isaac, "the son born by the power of the Spirit." The mistreatment of young Isaac by the teenager Ishmael became so irksome to Sarah that she insisted to Abraham that Hagar and Ishmael had to go! Paul quotes Sarah's demand of Abraham recorded in Genesis 21:10: "Get rid of the slave woman and her son, for the slave woman's son will never share in the

*"Get rid of the slave woman and her son, for the slave
woman's son will never share in the inheritance
with the free woman's son." (4:30)*

inheritance with the free woman's son." Although the matter distressed Abraham, God agreed with Sarah and advised Abraham, "Listen to whatever Sarah tells you, because it is through Isaac that your offspring will be reckoned" (Genesis 21:12).

Paul earlier told the Galatians, "Understand, then, that those who believe are children of Abraham" (3:7). Abraham's true offspring are all believers in the Christ who came from Isaac's line—not from Ishmael's. Paul makes the connection for the Galatians when he says, "Therefore, brothers, we are not children of the slave woman, but of the free woman."

Paul's point obviously extends far beyond dealing only with Ishmael. Recall that allegorically Ishmael stands for the Judaizers, and expelling "Ishmael," as Sarah did with God's approval, is the only appropriate solution also in Galatia. One could paraphrase Paul's implied advice: "Get rid of the Judaizers and their followers, for these people enslaved to the law will never share in the inheritance that comes as a gift to those who trust in God's gospel promises."

PART THREE
PAUL EXPLAINS SANCTIFICATION— HOW THE JUSTIFIED SINNER IS TO LIVE BEFORE GOD
(GALATIANS 5:1–6:10)

As we begin this third major part of Paul's letter, it may be useful to review the general outline of the letter. The six chapters of the letter divide themselves into three parts of two chapters each.

In the first two chapters we heard Paul defend his status as a true apostle, equal with the other apostles commissioned at Christ's ascension. That was not an ego trip for Paul, but rather, it established the truthfulness and reliability of the message he had brought to the Galatians.

What was Paul's message? This is detailed in chapters 3 and 4, particularly in how his message differs from the message urged by the false-teaching Judaizers, who had broken into the Galatian congregations and were misleading and unsettling Paul's recent converts to Christianity.

Paul had preached that a person is saved by grace alone, grace shown in God's keeping his promise and sending Jesus of Nazareth as the promised Messiah. This Savior lived a perfect life to fulfill what God's holy law rightly demanded of us, and he died an innocent death as our Substitute to pay for the countless sins and misdeeds with which we transgressed God's holy will.

On the basis of what Christ has done, God now credits Christ's merits to the sinner purely as a gift. He *justifies*, that is, he declares the sinner to be just. He looks at the sinner as if he were sinless, holy, and righteous.

This precious gift of the forgiveness of sins, peace with God, and a good conscience comes to sinners by faith. Faith is nothing other than trusting and believing God's promise— taking God at his word when he says, In Christ you are my dear children and heirs of eternal salvation.

That is the faith Abraham had, and "it was credited to him as righteousness." That is the faith God engendered also in the Galatians by Paul's preaching the good news to them. The gospel works such faith that takes God at his word and relies solely on his promise to give every good and blessing without any contribution from people or merit on their part.

But the Judaizers challenged the Galatians' simple faith in God's grace. They said, In addition to accepting Christ you must also follow the Old Testament ceremonies, since that has always been the way of God's people.

Alternating between strong, emotional rebuke and warm, winsome words, using both parable and allegory, Paul made this point: The law has been fulfilled and the ceremonies have been abolished. There is nothing you can or need to do. You have been freed from all legal requirements.

But that raises this question: Can Christians do anything they please? Are there no guidelines? The question is essentially one that asks how justified children of God are to live and put their "freedom" into practice. Paul addresses that point next.

Encouragements that flow from the doctrine of justification

Stand firm in your Christian liberty

5 **It is for freedom that Christ has set us free. Stand firm, then, and do not let yourselves be burdened again by a yoke of slavery.**

²Mark my words! I, Paul, tell you that if you let yourselves be circumcised, Christ will be of no value to you at all. ³Again I declare to every man who lets himself be circumcised that he is obligated to obey the whole law. ⁴You who are trying to be justified by law have been alienated from Christ; you have fallen away from grace. ⁵But by faith we eagerly await through the Spirit the righteousness for which we hope. ⁶For in Christ Jesus neither circumcision nor uncircumcision has any value. The only thing that counts is faith expressing itself through love.

To stand firmly in God's good graces without having to do anything to merit or earn this blessing—that is freedom indeed! For such freedom Christ has set us sinners free by his merit, which comes to us through faith. What folly to give up that freedom and once more take up the burden of trying to keep legal regulations, whether they be the Mosaic Law or any other pattern of works done to please God and thus earn his favor. Well does Paul urge the Galatians, and us: "It is for freedom that Christ has set us free. Stand firm, then, and do not let yourselves be burdened again by a yoke of slavery."

In the Galatians' case the "yoke of slavery" meant keeping Old Testament ceremonial regulations. Many individual precepts and regulations governed every phase of Jewish life: diet, dress, social customs, public life, worship, etc.

Although Gentile converts to Judaism, or proselytes, agreed to these precepts and regulations in principle, there seem to have been different levels of how completely they actually kept the individual rules. One thing is certain: to become full-fledged converts to Judaism, Gentiles would have to pledge to keep all the Mosaic regulations, and for males that meant accepting circumcision.

In this section when Paul speaks of the Galatians accepting circumcision, he is directing his remarks against those "who are trying to be justified by law" (verse 4)—those, that is, who considered this rite necessary for salvation. Hence Paul equates accepting circumcision with renouncing Christianity and converting to the outmoded Judaism of the Old Testament.

In verses 2 to 4 Paul gives three somewhat similar but overlapping reasons why the Galatian Christians should not accept circumcision:

1. It effectively negates Christ's sacrifice;
2. It obligates a person to keep the whole law;
3. It deprives a person of God's grace and thus puts him on his own, that is, on the "merit plan" of salvation.

Summoning the full authority of his apostolic office, Paul warns: "Mark my words! I, Paul, tell you that if you let yourselves be circumcised, Christ will be of no value to you at all. Again I declare to every man who lets himself be circumcised that he is obligated to obey the whole law. You who are trying to be justified by law have been alienated from Christ; you have fallen away from grace."

Falling away from grace means no longer being connected by faith to the God who graciously gives us all things as a gift. It means we're "going it alone" and that on judgment day we will have to take our chances with our own righteousness for acceptance before God's bar of justice.

That approach, in which we are "alienated from Christ," is worlds removed from what the Galatians learned from Paul's gospel, which the apostle here summarizes, "But by faith we eagerly await through the Spirit the righteousness for which we hope."

If it is by faith in Christ, by trusting God's promise, and not by our own performance that we "await . . . righteousness," then it makes no difference whether a person is circumcised or not. If the Galatians want to accept circumcision as a matter of choice and not as a requirement for salvation, that is their privilege. If they choose not to be circumcised, that too, despite the Judaizers' stern threats, is a privilege they may exercise. However, they must always remember "in Christ Jesus neither circumcision nor uncircumcision has any value. The only thing that counts is faith expressing itself through love."

The last phrase of this verse forms the transition to a new thought that will be the emphasis in this closing portion of the letter to the Galatians. The apostle has been talking about justification, how a person becomes right with God. He has clearly and forcefully stated that the only way a person can be right with God is to accept the righteousness God himself has prepared through the perfect life and innocent death of his Son. Since that righteousness comes in the form of a promise from a gracious God, the only way it can be received is by trusting and believing the God who has made the promise. Or as Paul puts it, "the only thing that counts is faith." As far as justification is concerned, the only thing that counts is faith. But note that Paul doesn't end his sentence in quite that way. He says, "The only thing that counts is faith *expressing itself through love*."

Faith alone saves, but saving faith is never alone. It is always "expressing itself through love." Appreciation for the unspeakably great grace God has shown us requires a response from us. It can't be any different. We simply have to say thank you to our God by doing deeds of love wherever and whenever an opportunity presents itself. Living this life of appreciative love is what is called sanctification. Sanctification, faith expressing itself in love, will be Paul's emphasis in the closing portion of the letter, but first he takes one more opportunity to warn against the Judaizers. Drawing his imagery from the athletic field, Paul tells the Galatians:

> **⁷You were running a good race. Who cut in on you and kept you from obeying the truth? ⁸That kind of persuasion does not come from the one who calls you. ⁹"A little yeast works through the whole batch of dough." ¹⁰I am confident in the Lord that you will take no other view. The one who is throwing you into confusion will pay the penalty, whoever he may be. ¹¹Brothers, if I am still preaching circumcision, why am I still being persecuted? In that case the offense of the cross has been abolished. ¹²As for those agitators, I wish they would go the whole way and emasculate themselves!**

The Galatians' good start was spoiled by the Judaizers, who tripped them up. These false teachers "cut in" on them and made them tentative and unsure in their race of faith. That kind of running was not what they learned from the Holy Spirit working through the gospel Paul preached to them.

As Paul thinks about the hurdles and obstacles put before his newly converted Galatians, he becomes indignant. He threatens, "The one who is throwing you into confusion will pay the penalty, whoever he may be."

It's interesting to note how little Paul tells us about the Judaizers, other than to condemn their false teaching. He never addresses any of them by name. Indeed, we don't learn from the letter whether the Judaizers were still in the Galatian congregations or whether they had moved on to other of Paul's congregations, leaving confusion and unrest in their wake. Nor does Paul tell us how many Judaizers there were. Paul speaks rather vaguely here, and in the singular, when he says, "The one who is throwing you into confusion will pay the penalty, whoever he may be." It may be hard to know or assess the damage now, but judgment day will set matters right, whoever the offenders may be.

Paul gives us only a hint regarding the personal attack the Judaizers were mounting against him. It would seem they had accused Paul of being inconsistent, in that he still sometimes "[preached] circumcision." Such a charge might have been based on Paul's willingness to have Timothy circumcised so he could be helpful in working with Jews (Acts 16:3) and his refusing to have Titus circumcised when his situation became a test case regarding the necessity of observing Old Testament rites and ceremonies (Galatians 2:3).

We don't know the details of their charge, but Paul hotly denies it as being not only inaccurate, but foolish and illogical as well. "If I am still preaching circumcision," Paul asks, "why am I still being persecuted? In that case the offense of the cross has been abolished." Continuing opposition from the Judaizers with their insistence on circumcision was eloquent testimony that Paul had never "caved in" on the matter of circumcision.

At this point Paul allows himself a bitter, almost coarse, outburst against the Judaizers when he suggests, "As for those agitators, I wish they would go the whole way and emasculate themselves!" If they're so bent on circumcision, so quick with the knife, Paul says, why don't they just go all the way and emasculate themselves! Obviously, Paul is being sharp, even sarcastic, to make a point. He is not offering a serious suggestion.

Walk in the spirit, not in the flesh

We have previously characterized Galatians as a letter that shows rapid and wide mood swings on the part of its author. Here again we see Paul shifting gears. After an emotional, no-holds-barred exchange with the errorists, Paul now switches to a much warmer tone of voice. He addresses his beloved Galatians as "my brothers." He warns them most tenderly and earnestly against a problem that might result if they don't listen carefully to and analyze properly the rebuttal he has just made to the Judaizers' position.

Paul has taken great pains to point out that salvation is a free gift that comes purely by grace through faith in Christ and his redemptive work done in our stead. The demands of the law can make no claims on us. We are perfectly free and need not do anything in order to be saved.

That freedom from the law and its demands could, however, be misunderstood as total license and liberty, giving the Galatians permission to do just as they please in their daily lives. Paul anticipates this possible misunderstanding and heads it off.

¹³You, my brothers, were called to be free. But do not use your freedom to indulge the sinful nature; rather, serve one another in love. ¹⁴The entire law is summed up in a single command: "Love your neighbor as yourself." ¹⁵If you keep on biting and devouring each other, watch out or you will be destroyed by each other.

A key term in this section is the Greek word translated as "the sinful nature." Literally it means "flesh" and refers to our unregenerate self—what we are by nature in our fallen and sinful state, commonly called our "old Adam."

The old Adam is totally selfish and self-centered. Any freedom from restraint is going to be interpreted by him as an opportunity to throw off authority, grab what he can for himself, and indulge his every whim and pleasure. In short, the "flesh" is that part of us and our nature that wants to do just as it pleases, without thinking of anybody else. That is its idea of "freedom."

But Paul warns, "Do not use your freedom to indulge the sinful nature; rather, serve one another in love. The entire law is summed up in a single command: 'Love your neighbor as yourself.'"

To be sure, Christ has fulfilled every demand of the law and there remains nothing for us to do to earn salvation. But when we realize that salvation has been earned for us and that everything has come to us as a free gift of God's grace, then we will want to show our appreciation to our gracious God for so great a gift. And if we, as redeemed children of God, now cast about to discover what would please such a God and what we can do to show our appreciation to God, then God's law gives us guidance and direction. It indicates what God would have us do.

Paul turns to Leviticus for a summary statement of God's holy and unchangeable will, his "law." The verse Paul chooses is, "Love your neighbor as yourself," which is nothing other than God's directive to serve one another in love. It's what Paul has already previously referred to as "faith expressing itself through love" (5:6).

Paul undergirds the practical value of keeping God's command by pointing out the damaging effect of not keeping it and operating with a lack of love. "If you keep on biting and devouring each other, watch out or you will be destroyed by each other." But avoiding the bad effects of lovelessness is not the real motivation to show love for one's neighbor. The true and proper motivation has to come from quite a different source, the new spiritual life worked in the believer by the Holy Spirit.

[16]"So I say, live by the Spirit, and you will not gratify the desires of the sinful nature. [17]For the sinful nature desires what is contrary to the Spirit, and the Spirit what is contrary to the

sinful nature. They are in conflict with each other, so that you do not do what you want. ¹⁸But if you are led by the Spirit, you are not under law.

In the previous paragraph "flesh," or "sinful nature," was a key term. Its counterpart needs to be noted in this section. It's the word rendered "Spirit" in the NIV translation. That term can properly be written with a capital *S* and will then be understood to refer to the Holy Spirit. But it also can be rendered with a lowercase *s* and refer to the spiritual nature, the new man worked in believers when they come to faith in Christ. In fact, in passages where "flesh" and "spirit" are contrasted or pitted against each other, the lowercase "spirit" or "spiritual nature" often seems preferable.

A moment's reflection will show, however, that the distinction is not of as great a consequence as it might at first appear. There can be no spiritual life unless the Spirit has first worked that life in the believer (1 Corinthians 12:3). And, on the other hand, where the Spirit is active in a person's life, there will inevitably be spiritual life and a new spiritual nature (John 3:6).

In the present context a practical balance between the two meanings can be struck by understanding the first and last uses of the term (verses 16,18) as referring to the Holy Spirit, and the two uses in between as speaking of the spiritual nature of a Christian. Such an adjustment will have our translation of these verses coming out something like this: "So I say, live under the guiding influence of the *Holy Spirit*, and you will not gratify the desires of your sinful nature. For the old sinful nature desires what is contrary to your new *spiritual life*. And the new *spiritual life*, in turn, is contrary to your old, original sinful nature. These two natures are in conflict with each other, so that, as a Christian who at all times

97

retains an old Adam alongside your new man, you find yourself not doing what you want. But if you are led by the *Holy Spirit*, you are not under law but rather in sync with it."

Paul explains that the Christian's life will always be a pitched battle. There is an ongoing conflict between what the rebellious old Adam wants to do contrary to God's will and what the new man, guided by the Spirit, wants to do in accordance with God's will.

What these two entities in the Christian want to do is light-years apart. The difference is immediately apparent as one observes their activities. Paul lists the negative side first. He says, "The acts of the sinful nature are obvious," and he then proceeds to lay out a scandalous catalog of vices.

[19]The acts of the sinful nature are obvious: sexual immorality, impurity and debauchery; [20]idolatry and witchcraft; hatred, discord, jealousy, fits of rage, selfish ambition, dissensions, factions [21]and envy; drunkenness, orgies, and the like. I warn you, as I did before, that those who live like this will not inherit the kingdom of God.

Paul names 15 crass sins and ends the series by adding "and the like." He could no doubt have named more. And for that matter, a shorter list would have been just as incriminating. The point is that nothing good comes from our old, sinful nature.

A careful look at the placement of semicolons in the NIV translation indicates that the translators have attempted to group the vices. "Sexual immorality, impurity and debauchery" are sins against the Sixth Commandment. "Idolatry and witchcraft" are infractions of the First and Second Commandments. "Hatred, discord, jealousy, fits of rage, selfish ambition, dissensions, factions and envy" are sins against the neighbor, essentially a breaking of the Fifth Commandment. "Drunkenness" and "orgies" lump together all manner of intemperance.

Paul doesn't elaborate. He simply states, "I warn you, as I did before, that those who live like this will not inherit the kingdom of God." It is important to keep in mind that Christ died also for sins like those on Paul's list. The apostle is not saying they are unforgivable. After all, in their pagan past the Galatians had done all of them. Paul previously had to preach against such wickedness in their lives. Forgiven of their past, the Galatians, however, dare not blithely return to their pet sins. They know from Paul's gospel that God's Son came down from heaven to give his life as a ransom for sin. If God is that serious about sin, how can the Galatians, or we, carelessly continue in a sinful lifestyle? That would be a contradiction in terms. That would not be faith expressing itself in love toward God or our neighbor.

Paul is not speaking of individual lapses into sin that the Christian repents of and receives forgiveness for. Paul is speaking of a pattern, a consistent and persistent lifestyle. The original Greek makes that plain. Literally Paul says, "Those *continuing to do things of that sort* will not inherit the kingdom of God."

²²But the fruit of the Spirit is love, joy, peace, patience, kindness, goodness, faithfulness, ²³gentleness and self-control. Against such things there is no law. ²⁴Those who belong to Christ Jesus have crucified the sinful nature with its passions and desires.

Quite different from the "acts of the sinful nature" are the lives and activities of those who walk in the Spirit. Again Paul gives us a list, this time of things that mark (or *should* mark) the Christian life. Like the acts of the sinful nature, these actions too are "obvious." They're observable in the day-to-day life of the child of God.

Note, however, a difference in how Paul describes the two sets of activities. The "acts of the sinful nature" are things that sinful people can do by themselves. They need no help. The good things, on the other hand, are not things that come naturally. They are the "fruit of the Spirit." God the Holy Spirit produces them in and through us.

As he did with the negatives, Paul now lines up the positives in a list. This time there are nine items. Attempts have been made to group these also. It's fair to say that the first item, "love," really embraces all the rest and could stand by itself. Scripture gives warrant for that when it says that love is the fulfillment of the whole law (Romans 13:10; see also 1 Corinthians 13:4-6).

If one wants to see a pattern, it would seem that three groups of three virtues yield a workable scheme. The first three, "love, joy, peace," are inner qualities that reflect our Christian relationship to God. The next three, "patience, kindness, goodness," show themselves in the Christian's attitude and actions toward his neighbor. The last three, "faithfulness, gentleness and self-control" reflect how the new man conducts himself in view of the duties, opportunities, and obligations that come to him in his Christian calling.

When Paul says, "Against such things there is no law," he is using a figure of speech called a litotes. In a litotes the writer uses a major understatement to make an important point. Not only is there no law against the good Christian virtues Paul enumerates, but these virtues are highly desirable! They are what God wants. Such attitudes and actions in the Christian conform completely to God's holy will.

These qualities, in ever-increasing measure, show themselves in the Christian life. People whom the Holy Spirit has brought to faith in Christ have renounced their old sinful past. So complete is this break that Paul can say, "Those who belong to Christ Jesus have crucified the sinful nature with its passions and desires." Hence not the "acts of the sinful nature," but the "fruit of the Spirit" is the hallmark of the Christian life.

²⁵Since we live by the Spirit, let us keep in step with the Spirit.

We have previously indicated that the original Greek does not determine for us whether the author intended a capital *S* "Spirit" or lowercase "spirit." The context must help us determine that. In this verse the NIV translators have chosen "Spirit" both times the term is used. That is not an impossible interpretation. It does, however, seem a little redundant and doesn't give much progression of thought from the first half of the verse to the second half. "Living by the Spirit" seems to be almost the same as "keeping in step with the Spirit."

A somewhat likelier thought progression suggests itself if one takes the first use of the term in the sense of "spirit" or the "spiritual life" that characterizes believers in Christ Jesus, who have crucified their old sinful nature. The verse would then say, Since by faith we have this new spiritual nature dwelling in us, let us keep in step with the Holy Spirit, who created and made that new life possible.

Be considerate of the weak and erring

²⁶Let us not become conceited, provoking and envying each other.
6 Brothers, if someone is caught in a sin, you who are spiritual should restore him gently. But watch yourself, or you also may be tempted. ²Carry each other's burdens, and in this way you will fulfill the law of Christ. ³If anyone thinks he is

101

something when he is nothing, he deceives himself. ⁴Each one should test his own actions. Then he can take pride in himself, without comparing himself to somebody else, ⁵for each one should carry his own load.

Although the words Paul wrote to the Galatians are inspired and inerrant, the chapter and verse divisions of the letter are not of divine origin but of a later human arrangement, designed merely to make it easier for us to locate specific passages. Hence we need not be bound by these divisions. We have therefore chosen to put 5:26 with the opening five verses of chapter 6.

In this section Paul is giving advice regarding the delicate matter of interpersonal relations. When we recall the situation that occasioned this letter, we can appreciate the fact that the Galatian congregations had a great deal of patching up to do. If Paul's letter is heeded by all the readers, some of them will have to back down from their previously held position. And others will need to let them back down as quietly and painlessly as possible.

Paul urges considerate treatment of the weak and erring. Those who were misled and temporarily held to a wrong position would feel chagrin. How easy it would have been for those who were on the right side of the Judaizing question to become conceited by their having been right all along. If they obnoxiously rubbed it in, they would undoubtedly provoke the others.

Paul is not restricting himself just to problems with Judaizing, however. He speaks in general terms when he writes, "Brothers, if someone is caught in a sin, you who are spiritual should restore him gently. But watch yourself, or you also may be tempted. Carry each other's burdens, and in this way you will fulfill the law of Christ."

Paul is putting oil on troubled waters here as he winds down his letter and waits for favorable results from it. He uses the winsome term "brothers" in addressing the Galatians. Tactfully, he prefaces his advice with the conditional clause "*If* someone is caught in a sin"—or as it could also be translated, "*Whenever* someone is caught in a sin." Paul is not coming down hard on those who need help. Neither should the strong brothers, the "spiritual" Galatians.

But the strong Christians *are* to help the weak. Sin detected in a brother's life dare not be ignored. It needs to be rebuked and repented of. The brother's spiritual health needs to be "restored." (See Matthew 18:15: "If he listens to you, you have won your brother over.") The correctors, however, are to render this service "gently."

Paul again uses picture language when he urges, "Carry each other's burdens." Correcting and admonishing a brother is not lording it over him. It is helping him. It is sharing a burden, making it our own and showing a genuine concern about it, so that in a real sense we are joining him in carrying it.

"In this way you will fulfill the law of Christ," the apostle says. We need to keep two things in mind so as not to misunderstand Paul here. "Law" does not in this instance mean a "legal requirement," but rather a "pattern," a model to follow. Furthermore, the new man in the Christian does not follow Christ's pattern to earn favor or merit with God; rather, he acts out of appreciation for all that his gracious God has done for him. Paul uses much the same encouragement with the Ephesians when he writes, "Be kind and compassionate to one another, forgiving each other, just as in Christ God forgave you" (4:32).

Not only is the strong brother's kindness and consideration important for the weaker brother, but such action is important for the strong brother also. If he would act otherwise, he would in fact jeopardize his own spiritual status. Paul sounds both a note of caution and suggests a useful procedure: "If anyone thinks he is something when he is nothing, he deceives himself. Each one should test his own actions. Then he can take pride in himself, without comparing himself to somebody else, for each one should carry his own load."

The temptation is always there for the strong brother to compare himself to the weaker brother and then feel smug in his relatively greater strength. As an antidote to such an unwarranted approach Paul reminds us that "each one should carry his own load." We must all individually give account of ourselves before a righteous and holy God. Paul wrote to the Corinthians, "We must all appear before the judgment seat of Christ, that each one may receive what is due him for the things done while in the body, whether good or bad" (2 Corinthians 5:10).

In view of that day of reckoning, "each one should test his own actions." That means measuring ourselves not against the conduct of weak and fallible sinners, but against God's holy and just law. That law demands perfection. That law looks not only at deeds and actions, but at thoughts and motives as well. That law makes the observation that out of the heart come "evil thoughts, sexual immorality, theft, murder, adultery," etc. (Mark 7:21).

Each one should test his own actions, Paul advises. There is something of an edge on his words when he continues, "Then he can take pride in himself." Actually, he means just the opposite! Look at yourself in the mirror of God's holy law, Paul says, and you will see absolutely no basis for pride. You will see only sins and shortcomings, and you will feel shame and remorse over your shabby record. You will realize that you daily need God's grace and mercy just as much as the "weaker" brother does, to whom you were originally inclined to feel superior.

General admonitions

Paul's main purpose in writing the letter to the Galatians was to address the confusion caused by the Judaizers. They insisted that in addition to believing in Christ, the Galatians also had to observe the Law of Moses with its rites and ceremonies. Paul counters that with a ringing defense of salvation by faith alone, without the addition of any law-works. Paul followed that with the double encouragement to stand fast in their freedom from the law but not to use this freedom as a license to sin. He then moved on to encourage them to show considerate treatment toward any brothers who may still have some difficulty grasping the doctrinal significance of all this and applying it to their everyday lives.

Paul now moves on to more general encouragements, not tied directly to the doctrine of justification.

Encouragement to support messengers of the gospel

⁶Anyone who receives instruction in the word must share all good things with his instructor.

Paul lays on the Galatian congregations the obligation to care for the physical needs of their workers. "Anyone who receives instruction in the word," he says, "must share all good things with his instructor." Recall that after Paul started a congregation, he would put local congregational leaders in charge and then move on to another location (Acts 14:21-23). Undoubtedly such leaders were serving the congregations of Galatia when Paul wrote this letter. It is these local leaders in the congregations, call them "pastors" if you will, of whom Paul is speaking.

Paul was very firm on the principle that the person who bears the gospel message to others has the right to expect material support from the people to whom he is bringing that message. (See 1 Corinthians 9:3-11.) For himself Paul chose not to take support (1 Corinthians 9:12,15), preferring rather to earn his own living by tentmaking (Acts 18:1-3; 20:33-35). But Paul did not require or expect other ministers of the gospel to follow his pattern of not taking support. Nor does he allow congregations to force their ministers to follow his pattern. Paul insists that congregations support their church workers.

It is interesting to hear Paul refer to the money and material possessions congregations are to share with their church workers as "good things." From time to time movements in the church have extolled poverty and considered it a virtue. Speaking by inspiration, Paul does not reflect that view. Money and property are "good things," a gift from the Lord. It's not a sin to be rich. The sin lies in improper use of wealth—and that can happen in any number of ways. At one end of the spectrum lies the nonuse of material things: having them and hoarding them, and letting them be the goal of one's life. That is the sort of greed Paul calls "idolatry" (Ephesians 5:5). At the other end lies the reckless and indulgent squandering on self with no thought for others. Paul cautions against both misuses and warns that they will not go undetected by God.

7Do not be deceived: God cannot be mocked. A man reaps what he sows. 8The one who sows to please his sinful nature, from that nature will reap destruction; the one who sows to please the Spirit, from the Spirit will reap eternal life. 9Let us not become weary in doing good, for at the proper time we will reap a harvest if we do not give up.

Paul, good teacher that he is, again helps us see his point by using picture language. This time the picture is sowing and harvesting. How a person uses ("sows") the material things God gives will determine which outcome ("harvest") he experiences. If a person's sinful nature makes the decisions as to how wealth and property are used, then his actions will be totally selfish and self-serving. Such a person, with no thought for God or God's creatures, will come to a bad end. He "will reap destruction." (See the parable of the rich man and Lazarus—Luke 16:19-31.) Conversely, the person whose new man "sows to please the Spirit, from the Spirit will reap eternal life." (For a parallel thought, also using the picture of sowing and harvesting, see 2 Corinthians 8 and 9, particularly 9:6-11.)

In Paul's encouragement to the Galatians, as in many other places in Scripture, it is very important to realize that the activities he is discussing are the fruits of faith. The activity of proper "sowing" is not in and of itself the thing that leads to "reaping" eternal life. Rather, the "sowing" is a Christian's response, his proper use of the material things a gracious God has given him. The primary gifts of forgiveness of sin and a place in heaven are accepted by faith in Christ. That's always separate from and prior to the Christian's response. The Christian's subsequent activity of "sowing" is simply the proof, the outward indication, that living faith is at work in the Christian's life as he travels the road toward heaven.

Encouragement to do good to all, especially to believers

To people with a spiritual outlook created by the gospel Paul can give the encouragement:

[10]Therefore, as we have opportunity, let us do good to all people, especially to those who belong to the family of believers.

Recall that Paul began this section by encouraging the Galatians to be generous in sharing material "good things" with their church workers. Now he broadens that out considerably to include helping "all people" as opportunity allows. And he takes special care to include those who are closest, the members of the family—especially the family of believers. Paul expresses virtually the same thought in writing to Timothy: "If anyone does not provide for his relatives, and especially for his immediate family, he has denied the faith and is worse than an unbeliever" (1 Timothy 5:8). Notice also how proper use of material things is viewed as a fruit of faith, whereas misuse of them signals a lack of saving faith and makes one "worse than an unbeliever." Here is food for thought for many a "deadbeat dad" and for parents in general who neglect their children, as well as for children who neglect aging parents.

CONCLUSION
(GALATIANS 6:11-18)

In our day, writing material is readily available. It was not always so. Among the ancients, writing materials, such as parchment, vellum, and papyrus, were relatively scarce and expensive. Also the mechanics of writing were something of a specialized skill. The use of professional "scribes," or secretaries, was common practice.

Paul seems to have employed a scribe to whom he dictated his letters. At the close of Romans there is the interesting line "I, Tertius, who wrote down this letter, greet you in the Lord" (16:22).

It was a matter of concern to Paul that the recipients of his letters could be sure that the letters were authentic. We get a little insight into that concern when we hear Paul warn the Thessalonians, "Concerning the coming of our Lord Jesus Christ and our being gathered to him, we ask you, brothers, not to become easily unsettled or alarmed by some prophecy, report or *letter supposed to have come from us*, saying that the day of the Lord has already come" (2 Thessalonians 2:1,2).

It would appear that letters Paul had not written were being circulated as coming from him. To prove the authenticity of a scribe-written letter Paul would personally add a greeting and sign off with his name. That explains his remark at the close of 2 Thessalonians: "I, Paul, write this greeting in my own hand, which is the distinguishing mark in all my letters. This is how I write" (2 Thessalonians 3:17).

We seem to have such an authenticating feature here at the close of Paul's letter to the Galatians. He writes:

11See what large letters I use as I write to you with my own hand!

It is possible, of course, that the whole epistle was written in "large letters" and Paul comments on it here. It seems more likely, however, that the rest of the letter from this point on is in Paul's own hand. Apparently his handwriting stands in marked contrast to the neat and precise work of the professional scribe.

Just why Paul would have written with "large letters" remains something of a mystery. Because the apostle says that he first came to Galatia because of an illness (4:13) and then recalls that at his arrival the Galatians would have been willing to tear out their own eyes and give them to him (4:15), some have concluded that Paul had very poor eyesight and thus couldn't see well enough to form neat little letters.

Others have theorized, largely on the strength of Paul's remark about bearing "on my body the marks of Jesus" (6:17), that beatings and stonings had left Paul crippled and too clumsy for neat and precise writing.

The only safe thing is to admit that we don't know the circumstances surrounding the writing of this closing paragraph. The content of the paragraph, however, is perfectly clear. It's a summary in which Paul returns to the main point of the letter. He warns once more against the folly and danger of listening to the Judaizers and letting them spoil the law-free gospel he preached.

12Those who want to make a good impression outwardly are trying to compel you to be circumcised. The only reason they do this is to avoid being persecuted for the cross of Christ. 13Not even those who are circumcised obey the law, yet they want you to be circumcised that they may boast about your flesh.

In order to understand Paul's concluding evaluation of the situation in Galatia, it is essential that we be very clear on the nature of the problem caused by the Judaizers.

The Judaizers were people of Jewish extraction who accepted Jesus of Nazareth as the promised Messiah, the Christ. Hence they were "Christian" by virtue of their acceptance of Christ. Accepting Christ, however, put them in very bad graces with their Jewish countrymen, who looked at accepting Christ as undercutting the Law of Moses and the Jewish customs that were the underpinnings of their national and social life.

Such a perception of Christianity was not unique to the Judaizers in Galatia. Recall that when Paul returned to Jerusalem after his third missionary journey, James and the brothers of the Jerusalem congregation alerted Paul to a potential problem. They reported: "You see, brother, how many thousands of Jews have believed, and all of them are zealous for the law. They have been informed that you teach all the Jews who live among the Gentiles to turn away from Moses, telling them not to circumcise their children or live according to our customs" (Acts 21:20,21).

Note that James speaks of "thousands of Jews" who believe in Christ and thus have become Christians. But they had a major misunderstanding about Paul's work among the Gentiles. They saw Paul as virtually anti-Semitic, forbidding the practice of Jewish customs.

Such an assessment of the apostle's work was incorrect. Paul himself kept many Old Testament customs. He ceremonially fulfilled a vow by shaving his head (Acts 18:18). And on the return leg of his third missionary journey he was in a hurry to get to Jerusalem so that he might attend one of the three great pilgrim festivals, Pentecost (Acts 20:16). Paul never forbade people to follow Jewish customs—as long as they did it as a matter of choice, in Christian liberty. What Paul vigorously opposed was Christian converts being *compelled* to observe Mosaic regulations.

We need to be careful not to group the believers in James' congregation in Jerusalem with those who troubled the Galatians. The latter were thoroughly disreputable in their approach. The Judaizers in Galatia were not acting according to Christian convictions. Paul says, "The only reason they do this is to avoid being persecuted for the cross of Christ." When confronted and opposed by their Jewish countrymen for turning Christian and leading others to Christianity, they wanted to be able to defend themselves by saying: "No, we didn't let these Gentile converts bypass Judaism. They're adherents to the Law of Moses, as you can tell from their accepting circumcision." Paul's assessment is, "They want to make a good impression outwardly by compelling you to be circumcised." He charges the Judaizers with being theologically wrong and morally dishonest.

What's more, they were hypocrites. "Not even those who are circumcised [the Judaizers] obey the law, yet they want you to be circumcised that they may boast about your flesh." The context makes it clear that "those who are circumcised" were Jews who were circumcised and who also wanted the Galatians to put themselves under the Mosaic regulations and ceremonies by accepting the rite of circumcision. Paul is indignant that these people, who don't strictly keep the ceremonies themselves, should demand that the Galatians do so.

The situation Paul denounces is essentially parallel to what Jesus addressed with the Pharisees of his day. Of them Jesus said: "They do not practice what they preach. They tie up heavy loads and put them on men's shoulders, but they themselves are not willing to lift a finger to move them. Everything they do is done for men to see" (Matthew 23:3-5).

112

The Judaizers not only wanted to insulate themselves from persecution, but they'd want to look good in the process. They wanted to be able to "boast" in the accomplishment of having brought the Galatian Christians into obedience to the Law of Moses. Paul would have none of that!

¹⁴May I never boast except in the cross of our Lord Jesus Christ, through which the world has been crucified to me, and I to the world. ¹⁵Neither circumcision nor uncircumcision means anything; what counts is a new creation. ¹⁶Peace and mercy to all who follow this rule, even to the Israel of God.

One might have expected Paul to launch a full-scale attack against circumcision. He doesn't. Rather, he returns one last time to the core issue. Paul has consistently made this point: human accomplishment and merit can't help us before God. There is nothing we can do to save ourselves or contribute to our salvation. Accepting circumcision doesn't help. And for that matter, refusing to accept circumcision, in and of itself, isn't any help either. Nothing we can do improves our status before God. Sinners from birth, we are by nature lost and condemned creatures. We are blind, at enmity with God, dead in transgressions and sins. Such a situation requires a complete change. Or as the apostle puts it, "What counts is a new creation."

And that new creation is what happens when sinners come to faith in Christ. By faith they exchange their own filthy rags for the glorious garment of Christ's perfect righteousness. Clothed in this, sinners are forgiven, at peace with God, assured of an eternity of bliss with God in heaven. Until that time, they spend their days on earth in cheerful service to the God who gave them all this by grace, freely as a gift. That is "faith expressing itself through love" (5:6).

Paul wrote much the same to the Corinthians: "Therefore, if anyone is in Christ, he is a new creation; the old has gone, the new has come! All this is from God, who reconciled us to himself through Christ" (2 Corinthians 5:17,18).

All this has come to the believer through Christ and his cross. Well might we all resolve with Paul: "May I never boast except in the cross of our Lord Jesus Christ." May we never boast in anything else; but also, may we *always* boast in the cross—and boast in it *alone*.

Boasting in Christ's cross brings great blessings, the blessings Paul requests for his readers when he prays, "Peace and mercy to all who follow this rule, even to the Israel of God." It will be immediately evident that when Paul speaks of "following this rule" he is not speaking of fulfilling a legal requirement. That would be contrary to everything he told the Galatians in his former preaching and in this letter. No, "following this rule" means accepting by faith the law-free gospel that gives everything as a free gift. All who trust in it are truly God's people. They are the real "Israel," not those who by circumcision put themselves under an outdated law code.

¹⁷Finally, let no one cause me trouble, for I bear on my body the marks of Jesus.

When someone talks a lot and theorizes and philosophizes on how things should be done, we may eventually tell such a person, "Put your money where your mouth is!" Paul has talked and written much, advancing a definite point of view and advocating a specific course of action. Paul's approach, however, was not like that of the Judaizers, who were not operating from sincere convictions but only wanted to look good and avoid persecution.

Paul may have stated his point forcefully, but it was a point he had been willing to espouse and defend, even at the cost of personal suffering and hardship (2 Corinthians 11:21-29). He had "put his money where his mouth is." He had endured beatings, a stoning, and persecution for Christ, and he bore the "marks," the scars, to prove it. Hence the Galatians could trust him as a reliable witness.

18The grace of our Lord Jesus Christ be with your spirit, brothers. Amen.

Paul had to write some sharp words to the Galatians because they were on the verge of following the wrong teachings of the Judaizers. But the Galatians had not fallen from grace. They had not become the enemy. They were his brothers, and he addresses them as such one last time.

On a number of occasions we have noted that the context has to determine whether to use a capital or lowercase *s* with the term "spirit." Here, in writing to the Galatians and speaking of "your spirit," Paul clearly is referring to the heart and mind, the inner being, of the Galatians. As his closing prayer Paul makes a special request. He asks that the grace of the Lord Jesus Christ might be with their spirit.

In light of the main thrust of this letter, Paul's prayer for grace is a most appropriate closing request to make for his beloved Galatian brothers. Paul has taken pains to emphasize that salvation comes to people, not by their own works, but solely by God's *grace*. God's grace, Paul would have us remember, is that quality in the heart and mind of God that makes him eager and willing to give good gifts—the greatest of which, of course, is eternal salvation.

Since salvation is by grace and rests on God's promises rather than on man's performance, it is absolutely sure and certain. Hence Paul can end his prayer and his letter with "Amen," that word of Christian confidence with which every believer says, "This will most certainly happen."

EPHESIANS
INTRODUCTION TO EPHESIANS

The apostle Paul wrote this letter to the Christians in Ephesus while he was a prisoner in Rome, about the year A.D. 61. Although these traditional assumptions have been challenged by modern critics, they still seem very plausible.

Author and Date

The author identifies himself as "Paul, an apostle of Christ Jesus" (1:1) and indicates he is a "prisoner" (3:1; 4:1), an "ambassador in chains" (6:20). Recall the events leading up to Paul's imprisonment: After returning from his third missionary journey, Paul went up to Jerusalem. There he fell under the wrath of orthodox Jews who thought he had brought Gentiles into the temple (Acts 21:17-36). Rescued from the Jewish mob by Roman soldiers, Paul found himself in the clutches of the Roman legal system. For two years he languished in prison in the provincial capital of Caesarea, where a corrupt Roman governor held him, hoping for a bribe (Acts 24:26,27). In frustration Paul appealed his case to the high court in Rome, the capital of the Roman Empire (Acts 25:1-12, particularly 9-12).

Although shipwrecked on the way to Rome (Acts 27), the apostle eventually arrived there safely. While under house arrest and awaiting trial, Paul was able to carry on a limited ministry to people who came to him. As part of his ministry he also corresponded with congregations, and four of his "captivity letters" are included in the New Testament: Ephesians, Colossians, Philemon, and Philippians.

An alternate explanation not favored by this writer is that Paul's captivity letters were written during his earlier impris-

Western Asia Minor

onment in Caesarea. Such a view does not change the content or value of these letters, however.

There is some leeway regarding the date of this and the other captivity letters. The dates for Paul's life and ministry are computed by matching what Scripture tells us about Paul's work with known dates from history. For example, Paul's work in Corinth coincided with the administration of the Roman proconsul Gallio (Acts 18:12). The change in provincial governorship from Felix to Festus—and the occasion for Paul's appealing to Rome—was about A.D. 60. Hence Paul's two-year imprisonment in Rome would have been about A.D. 61–63, give or take a year or two.

Recipients

The majority of Greek manuscripts and the consistent tradition of the early church indicate that this letter was addressed to the church in Ephesus.

In a few manuscripts the phrase "in Ephesus" is missing from the opening verse, and that has led some critics to question the letter being sent to that location. That leaves it addressed simply "To the saints, the faithful in Christ Jesus." The two most notable manuscripts that do not have "in Ephesus" are the capital-letter manuscripts designated as "Aleph" and "B." Until recently, those two manuscripts were given undue weight in evaluating manuscript evidence, but of late there has been something of a shift toward the more balanced view of considering *all* the manuscript evidence. When all the evidence is considered, the reading "in Ephesus" retains a secure place in the text.

A second objection is that in this letter Paul sent no personal greetings to individuals in Ephesus with whom he had worked closely. However, the same can be said of Paul's two letters to the Thessalonians. Paul had worked intensively

119

there just shortly before writing to them, and yet that letter includes no personal greetings. Note also that Paul had not visited the church in Rome before he penned Romans to them (1:10,13), yet he sent greetings by name to some two dozen people (Romans 16). The point is that the inclusion or noninclusion of greetings to individuals does not seem to form a very compelling basis for determining the destination of a Pauline epistle.

The assumption that underlies the commentary that follows is that Ephesians, while certainly intended ultimately for the whole church as part of the New Testament canon, was originally sent to the congregation in Ephesus. But again, we must add that differing opinions as to the letter's recipients in no way affect its continuing worth or validity.

The importance of the city of Ephesus

A look at Paul's mission methodology will show why Ephesus was important in Paul's—or, rather, God's—game plan. Paul's pattern was to take the gospel to places where it had not previously been preached (Romans 15:20). To do that, he would regularly seek out urban population centers, particularly those with a high concentration of synagogue worshipers. To these synagogue worshipers, gathered around the Old Testament Scriptures, Paul proclaimed the good news: The Messiah you've been waiting for is here; it's Jesus of Nazareth (Acts 17:1-3).

Invariably that message divided the congregation. Some, most often a minority, accepted the message, while the rest retained their traditional position and eventually forced the new Christians out of their synagogues. These then left to form their own new congregation.

Paul and his colleagues worked with the new congregation, but rather soon Paul moved on to another urban center, leaving the synagogue people as leaders of the new congregation since they were well trained in the Old Testament Scripture.

The new congregation drew largely from area Gentiles, reaching out to their urban neighbors and eventually to the suburbs and outlying areas. A case in point, and of special interest to us, is the progress of the Word in and around Ephesus. Luke tells us about the work there: "This went on for two years, so that all the Jews and Greeks who lived in the province of Asia heard the word of the Lord" (Acts 19:10).

Ephesus was a major population center in the Roman province of Asia (Asia Minor, modern Turkey). Already at the start of his second missionary journey Paul had his eyes on Ephesus as a place to work, but he was "kept by the Holy Spirit from preaching the word in the province of Asia" (Acts 16:6). We soon find out why. When God gave Paul his "Macedonian call," he made it clear that at this time Paul was to cross over into the continent of Europe (Acts 16:9).

However, at the close of this European tour (Philippi, Thessalonica, Berea, Athens, and Corinth; see Acts 16–18), Paul stopped off in Ephesus on his way back to Antioch. He left Aquila and Priscilla there and promised, "I will come back if it is God's will" (Acts 18:21).

On Paul's third missionary journey "God's will" allowed him to do what he had been wanting to do already on his second journey, that is, set up headquarters in Ephesus. That now became possible for him, and he spent the next three years there. That, incidentally, is Paul's longest stay in any city that Scripture informs us of. His activities there, including his close call with Demetrius and the silversmiths, are recorded in Acts 19. For Paul's moving farewell to the Ephesian elders, see Acts 20:13-35.

Occasion

We have previously noted that while under house arrest in Rome awaiting trial, Paul was able to carry on a limited gospel ministry. People came to him for counsel and advice, and he was able to respond in person or by letter.

A scenario such as the following seems to conform to what we learn from Scripture regarding the circumstances that surround the writing of Ephesians. Word has reached Paul of a dangerous heresy besetting another congregation in Asia Minor, the congregation in the city of Colosse. The Colossians are being urged to heed certain spiritual forces and powers that were supposedly helpful to those who revered them and hurtful to those who did not regard them properly. Paul counters this false teaching with a ringing defense of the surpassing greatness of Christ, in whom "God was pleased to have all his fullness dwell" (Colossians 1:19). If the Colossians have Christ, they need nothing else! Hence, the letter to the Colossians extols Christ as the incomparably great and glorious head of the church.

Lacking a postal system such as we take for granted, the letter would have to be hand-delivered. It was decided that a trusted colleague by the name of Tychicus would carry it to Colosse.

Another matter is weighing on Paul's mind, however. During his stay in Rome he came in contact with a runaway slave, Onesimus. This slave had deserted his Christian master, a certain Philemon, who apparently was a member of the congregation in Colosse. Onesimus has since repented of his former infidelity and become Christian. Moreover, he has become a valuable "runner" for the grounded apostle. Paul would like to keep his services, but feels obligated to return Onesimus to his master (Philemon 13,14). Hence Paul writes a second letter for Tychicus to carry. This one is to Philemon, urging him to show kindly treatment to Onesimus, whom Paul is sending back to Colosse in the company of Tychicus (Colossians 4:7,9).

In traveling to the interior of Asia Minor, the logical route for Tychicus and Onesimus to follow would take them through the port city of Ephesus. Paul sees an opportunity to send a letter also to his beloved Ephesians. Hence he writes the letter to the Ephesians, of which Tychicus is also the bearer (Ephesians 6:21).

Content

Much in Ephesians parallels what Paul wrote to the Colossians. The incomparably great power of God in Christ is still prominent, but with a twist. In Ephesians the focus is rather on what God's great power has done for his believers, the church. Thus, as Colossians stresses the greatness of Christ, who is the head of the church, so Ephesians elaborates on the church, of which Christ is the head.

The letter divides neatly into two sections. The first three chapters deal with the gracious plan of salvation that God conceived already in eternity, implemented in time, and which will reach its completion on judgment day, when God takes his believers to himself for an eternity of bliss in heaven. A prominent theme is that all this comes by grace, that is, as a free gift from God (note particularly 2:8-10).

The last three chapters outline the Christian's response to God's grace and enjoin a life of love and service to God and our neighbor. Along with other directives, Paul includes his Table of Duties for husbands and wives, children and parents, slaves and masters. Notable in this section is the thought that Christian marriage is a reflection of the love Christ has for his bride, the church.

Outline of Ephesians

Greeting 1:1,2

I. God's eternal plan of salvation 1:3–3:21
   A. A plan devised by the triune God from eternity 1:1-23
      1. The Father's gracious purpose 1:3-6
      2. The Father's plan accomplished by the Son's work 1:7-12
      3. The Father's plan sealed by the Holy Spirit 1:13,14

   Prayer that God enlighten the Ephesians to see his gracious power 1:15-23

   B. God's eternal plan of salvation was carried out in time 2:1-22
      1. Both Jews and Gentiles are saved by grace 2:1-10
      2. Jews and Gentiles are united into one church 2:11-22
   C. God's eternal plan of salvation was preached to Gentiles by Paul 3:1-21
      1. The "mystery" of God's grace revealed 3:1-6
      2. The mystery proclaimed by Paul 3:7-13

   Prayer that God enable the Ephesians to comprehend the love of Christ 3:14-21

II. The blessed effects of God's saving grace 4:1–6:20
   A. A life of holiness 4:1-6:9
      1. Holiness is to show itself in unity among believers 4:1-16
      2. Holiness is to show itself in living a pure life 4:17–5:20
      3. Holiness is to show itself in assuming responsibilities 5:21–6:9

GREETING
(EPHESIANS 1:1,2)

1 **Paul, an apostle of Christ Jesus by the will of God,**
To the saints in Ephesus, the faithful in Christ Jesus:
²Grace and peace to you from God our Father and the Lord Jesus Christ.

In writing to the Ephesians, Paul uses the standard form for ancient letters. The first two verses of his letter to the Ephesians do not form a sentence; they are a formula or pattern consisting of three parts. First the author identifies himself; next he indicates to whom he is writing; and then he adds an opening greeting.

The author of this epistle is Paul, originally known as Saul of Tarsus. Trained at the feet of Gamaliel, an eminent teacher in Jerusalem, Saul was a Pharisee and an avowed enemy of Christianity. In his zeal for traditional Judaism he persecuted Christians in Jerusalem and even in outlying regions. In the course of a raid on Christians in Damascus Saul was confronted in blinding light by the risen Christ, who demanded of him, "Saul, Saul, why do you persecute me?" (Acts 9:4).

Corrected of his folly and converted by the Spirit, Saul the persecutor became Paul the Christian. That, however, was obviously not Paul's own doing. It came about, he acknowledges, "by the will of God." But God was not content merely to have Paul as a Christian follower, a disciple and learner. God willed to have Paul serve as an apostle. An apostle, by definition, is someone who is "sent out," an ambassador, a representative who speaks for the one sending him. By God's will Paul speaks as an "apostle of Christ Jesus." Hence Paul's words have authority. The letter to follow may come from Paul's pen, but, regarding the content, Paul the apostle says, "This is what the Lord says."

Paul addresses his letter to "the saints in Ephesus, the faithful in Christ Jesus." In our day the term "saint" has taken on a somewhat different meaning from the one intended here. Common usage is inclined to attach the term to people who have died ("my sainted grandmother"), or people accord the term to someone whose conduct lifts him above the common run of men ("He's a real saint!").

Paul, however, intends more than that. Literally the term "saints" means "holy ones." And that is precisely how Paul regards his readers. If we look ahead to verse 4, we hear Paul say they are people whom God chose "before the creation of the world to be holy and blameless in his sight" (verse 4). That holiness and blamelessness, of course, can come only through the forgiveness of sins received by faith in Christ. Hence in this letter Paul is addressing believers. We might paraphrase his words, "To the believers in Ephesus who are holy by faith in Christ Jesus."

Because a few manuscripts do not contain the words "in Ephesus," some question whether it was intended for the congregation in Ephesus. The content of the letter, of course, is not affected by its destination. It remains God's inerrant, inspired message for all times and would remain so even if it were a general letter intended for a number of congregations, as modern interpreters tend to claim. It should be noted, however, that the majority of manuscript evidence going back to the earliest times and drawn from all quarters of the church favors inclusion of the words "in Ephesus."

The third element in Paul's salutation is the greeting itself. Paul combines two terms, "grace" and "peace," both standard greetings of the day.

The Greek word translated "grace" is the ordinary term one Greek person would use in greeting another. It's the word Matthew uses to record Gabriel's salutation to Mary when he announced to her that she would become the mother of our Lord. "Peace" is the standard Jewish secular greeting—the familiar Hebrew term "Shalom."

In Paul's context, however, both are much more than secular terms; they are the grace and peace that come from "God our Father and the Lord Jesus Christ." With the term "grace" Paul calls attention to an amazing quality in the heart and mind of God that makes him willing—yes, eager—to give. And a state of peace comes to the person who has received God's gracious gifts. The two elements of Paul's greeting to the Ephesians, therefore, go together as cause and effect. And by way of anticipation, let us note how combining the standard Greek and Jewish greetings and investing them with a new, spiritual meaning is the perfect introduction to a letter that will be saying much about how in Christ Jews and Gentiles have been brought together into one body, the Christian church.

PART ONE
GOD'S ETERNAL PLAN OF SALVATION
(EPHESIANS 1:3–3:21)

Paul's letters tend to divide roughly into two major parts. Although it is a bit simplistic, it is nonetheless useful to remind ourselves of this fact. In the first half of his letters he usually shares some important points of doctrine. Then in the second half of the letter he applies the doctrinal truth. He helps his readers answer the question: What does this doctrinal truth mean for me? The six chapters of Paul's letter to the Ephesians follow that basic division.

The overarching theme of the first major part is God's eternal plan of salvation. Under this general theme are three subdivisions, each presented in one of the first three chapters. The first chapter deals with God's saving plan as it was formed already in eternity in heaven. Some have called this "the divine side of church history." The second chapter deals with how God in the course of time sent his Son into the world to become true man and live and die as the sinner's Substitute, thus laying the basis for the Christian church. That has been referred to as "the human side of church history." The third chapter deals with "Paul's role in church history," namely, the task God gave him of bringing knowledge of the Savior to Gentiles and thus paving the way for the union of Jews and Gentiles into one "body," that is, the church.

A plan devised by the triune God from eternity

The terms "Trinity" and "triune" do not occur in the Bible, but the Scriptures leave no doubt that it is the triune God who has been active in procuring our salvation. In the opening chapter of Ephesians the three persons of the Trinity are clearly in evidence, for Paul by inspiration speaks of the Father's gracious purpose (verses 3-6), which was accomplished by the Son's work (verses 7-12) and sealed by the Holy Spirit (verses 13,14).

The Father's gracious purpose

³Praise be to the God and Father of our Lord Jesus Christ, who has blessed us in the heavenly realms with every spiritual blessing in Christ. ⁴For he chose us in him before the creation of the world to be holy and blameless in his sight. In love ⁵he predestined us to be adopted as his sons through Jesus Christ, in accordance with his pleasure and will—⁶to the praise of his glorious grace, which he has freely given us in the One he loves.

This section begins a doxology, a song of praise to God, which continues through verse 14. In the Greek it is all one sentence—some two hundred words. The NIV translators have broken it down into shorter sentences, but it's still fairly complex. Therefore, we have highlighted these main concepts. Keep an eye out for them.

1. From eternity God has had a plan of salvation.
2. This plan is fulfilled in and through Christ.
3. God's plan gives us unspeakably great and precious blessings and is our reason for praising him.

Verse 3 literally says, "Blessed be God . . . who has blessed us . . . with every spiritual blessing." The author speaks to and for people who realize how very fortunate they are. What makes them so fortunate is that they have received "every spiritual blessing." Not one good thing is missing. Everything connected with "the heavenly realms" is theirs. Precisely what those blessings are will be indicated later.

From whom did the recipients receive those blessings? Paul identifies the Giver as "the God and Father of our Lord Jesus Christ," who has blessed us "in Christ." Everything from God comes in Christ and only in Christ.

How important Christ is in the equation becomes evident when Paul declares, "for he [the Father] chose us in him [Christ] before the creation of the world to be holy and blameless in his sight." We have noted that God had a plan that existed already in his mind "before the creation of the world." In Christ, God chose us to be holy and blameless. It is not that we were holy and blameless to begin with, and for that reason God took a liking to us and chose us. No, far from it! He chose us when we had no righteousness to offer. In fact, he chose us before we were born, before the world even existed. God chose us, Paul says, not *because* we were holy and blameless, but he chose us "*to be* holy and blameless." He chose us—sinners that we are—in order to make us righteous in Christ. Every spiritual blessing rests on Christ and his saving merit.

God's choosing us from eternity is often referred to as "election." It can also be called "predestination," as Paul does when he continues, "In love he [the Father] predestined us to be adopted as his sons through Jesus Christ, in accordance with his pleasure and will."

Election and predestination are not two separate, unrelated things. In fact, Paul connects them here. We have called attention to the fact that this whole opening section is actually one long sentence. Instead of having two separate sentences here, in the Greek Paul puts the two expressions together in a way that might well be translated, "God chose us by predestining us to be adopted as his sons through Jesus Christ." Note the same combination in verse 11.

Think of what that says! From eternity, before time existed, God's plan was to make us members of his family, to bring us into his household as his sons and daughters. Hence, he is our Father and we are his children, in line for a full inheritance. Everything that God has is even now being used for our good and blessing, and it will visibly and tangibly become our personal possession in heaven.

Why does God do all that? "In love he predestined us," Paul says, "in accordance with his pleasure and will." We might simply say he did it because he wanted to do it. It was "his pleasure and will," prompted by his great love for us.

But Paul answers our question in yet another way. Recall that he began this section by directing the reader's attention to the God "who has blessed us . . . with every spiritual blessing in Christ." As we have seen, these spiritual blessings, which culminate in our adoption as God's sons and daughters, are totally undeserved. They come as a pure gift of God's grace. Why does God give them? So that we may be led to thank and praise him, or as Paul says, "to the praise of his glorious grace, which he has freely given us in the One he loves [Christ]." Note again, everything comes through Christ, the One whom the Father loves and with whom he is well pleased (Matthew 3:17).

The Father's plan accomplished by the Son's work

⁷In him we have redemption through his blood, the forgiveness of sins, in accordance with the riches of God's grace ⁸that he lavished on us with all wisdom and understanding. ⁹And he made known to us the mystery of his will according to his good pleasure, which he purposed in Christ, ¹⁰to be put into effect when the times will have reached their fulfillment—to bring

132

all things in heaven and on earth together under one head, even Christ.

¹¹In him we were also chosen, having been predestined according to the plan of him who works out everything in conformity with the purpose of his will, ¹²in order that we, who were the first to hope in Christ, might be for the praise of his glory.

In this section the emphasis shifts from election itself to the One through whom our election was made possible. The centrality of Christ, so evident in the previous section, becomes even more pointed and direct here. Note once more Paul's key concepts: God's eternal plan, fulfilled in Christ, for our good and blessing, so that we are led to thank and praise our gracious God.

What was earlier referred to in general terms as "every spiritual blessing" and then narrowed down a bit as our "adoption" into God's family now comes into sharp focus. Our greatest blessing, the apostle tells us, is the forgiveness of sins we have in Christ. "In him [Christ] we have redemption through his blood, the forgiveness of sins, in accordance with the riches of God's grace that he lavished on us with all wisdom and understanding."

Paul uses two terms that differ as to the picture underlying them yet are virtually interchangeable in meaning: "redemption" and "forgiveness." *Redemption* implies that someone is a slave or captive and needs to be ransomed. *Forgiveness* implies that someone has acted improperly toward another and in so doing has incurred guilt that needs to be covered over or taken away.

Both require the payment of a heavy price. The sinner has offended God himself; the price is—or at least should be— the sinner's life. "The wages of sin is death" (Romans 6:23). But "in accordance with the riches of God's grace that he lavished on us," he did the unthinkable: God himself paid the price. He sent his Son to be our substitute, to suffer and die in our place. Through his blood we have been rescued from the captivity of sin and freed from its guilt.

In a million years we would not have devised such a plan. Rather, God devised it "in accordance with the riches of [his] grace that he lavished on us with all wisdom and understanding."

Not only would we not have thought up a plan like this, but we would never have grasped or understood it if he had not "made known to us the mystery of his will according to his good pleasure, which he purposed in Christ." The "mystery" of God's will will be treated more fully later in this letter (3:2-13). Suffice it at this stage to say that the mystery of God's will is almost synonymous with God's plan of salvation, that is, his will to save sinners. God's plan is not mysterious in the sense that it mystifies people or is incomprehensible to them. It is a mystery only in the sense that people cannot come to understand it by themselves. God has to explain it to them and lead them to know it and accept it. And that he does, of course, in the gospel that proclaims his grace in Christ.

Although a fuller explanation of the mystery is coming in chapter 3, Paul does not leave us waiting until then without a clue. The mystery of God's will, Paul tells us, has as its purpose, "to bring all things in heaven and on earth together under one head, even Christ." Recall that in writing to the Colossians, Paul stresses the greatness of Christ, who is the head of the church. In Ephesians the same subject matter is treated, but from the other side. Here Paul talks much about the church, of which Christ is the head. However, not just the church but "all things in heaven and on earth" are to be brought together under Christ. Hence, we might say that in his letter to the Ephesians, Paul sets forth God's stated purpose and plan to bring all things in general, and the church in particular, under the headship of Christ. (See also verse 22.)

In speaking of how God's eternal plan centers on Christ, Paul returns once more to the subject of election and predestination. He states, "In him [Christ] we were also chosen, having been predestined according to the plan of him who works out everything in conformity with the purpose of his will, in order that we, who were the first to hope in Christ, might be for the praise of his glory."

When we hear such expressions as "predestined according to the plan" and "in conformity with the purpose of his will," we realize that nothing of which Paul speaks is happening by chance. Everything occurs exactly according to God's carefully foreordained plan, which was in place already in eternity.

In verses 4 and 5 Paul spoke in general terms about election and predestination. Now in verse 12 he narrows his focus and becomes specific about God's plan. Here Paul gives a clear indication of who the "we" are whom God chose. "We, who were the first to hope in Christ," are the people of the Jewish nation, among whom Paul includes himself.

In order to fulfill his promise of a Savior, given to Adam and Eve already in the Garden of Eden, God chose Abraham from out of all the families of the world and gave him three specific promises. God promised that he would make Abraham into a great nation, that his descendants would live in a special land, and that from the Jewish nation the Savior of the world would be born.

Before the world began, in keeping with his carefully laid out plan, God chose the descendants of Abraham, the Jewish nation, as his own special people. And in time he carried out that plan, as Paul's readers clearly understood. Why did God

135

do that? Paul answers, "In order that we, who were the first to hope in Christ, might be for the praise of his glory."

God's faithfulness to his promise, his reliability in sticking with his plan, and his patience with rebellious Israel serve to magnify God's glory. Well might Paul urge his readers, "Praise be to the God and Father of our Lord Jesus Christ" (verse 3).

God's faithfulness to the Jewish nation was only part of his plan, though. Paul hints at that when he says, "We . . . were the *first* to hope in Christ," implying there are others. We Jews may have been the first to believe in Christ, Paul says— but he quickly adds, "You [Ephesian readers, Gentiles by birth] also were included in Christ when you heard the word of truth, the gospel of your salvation." The Jews are part of God's plan, but in Christ the Gentiles are also in the picture. Note the implications of that for God's plan and purpose of bringing "all things in heaven and on earth together under one head, even Christ."

The Father's plan sealed by the Holy Spirit

[13]And you also were included in Christ when you heard the word of truth, the gospel of your salvation. Having believed, you were marked in him with a seal, the promised Holy Spirit, [14]who is a deposit guaranteeing our inheritance until the redemption of those who are God's possession—to the praise of his glory.

We have noted that the grand plan Paul is setting forth in his letter to the Ephesians involves all three persons of the Trinity. From eternity God the Father chose the elect in Christ. But that eternal counsel of God, centering in Christ, finds its fulfillment in time—when the Holy Spirit does his special work of bringing people to faith in Christ through the message of the gospel.

136

Paul directs our attention to this work of the Spirit when he shifts the spotlight from the grace God has shown to the Jews to the equal grace God has shown to the Gentiles. Paul sets the Gentile Ephesian believers alongside Jewish believers when he declares, "And you also were included in Christ when you heard the word of truth, the gospel of your salvation."

Not only has the Holy Spirit brought the Ephesians to faith, but his presence in their hearts serves yet another purpose. "Having believed," Paul says, "you were marked in him [Christ] with a seal, the promised Holy Spirit." The Ephesians bear a seal: having the Holy Spirit in their hearts. In ancient times a seal was the sign of ownership. For a Christian to bear the seal of the Holy Spirit is an indicator that he or she belongs to God. That is a *present* blessing.

But Paul points to yet another blessing coming from the Spirit's presence in our hearts by faith. We have assurance for the *future*. The apostle describes the Spirit as "a deposit guaranteeing our inheritance until the redemption of those who are God's possession."

A deposit, a down payment, is the first installment of a transaction and guarantees the rest of the obligation will also be met. The fact that God has given his Holy Spirit into our hearts by faith at the present time is an assurance that the rest of God's promise will also be forthcoming. It is his guarantee that he'll hold our inheritance in heaven for us "until the redemption [the final deliverance] of those who are God's possession." For a parallel passage that speaks of the Holy Spirit, both as a seal indicating God's present ownership of the believer and as the guarantee of future blessings with God in heaven, see 2 Corinthians 1:21,22.

Once again, for the third time in this section, Paul tells us why God has showered us with all these blessings: to give us cause to thank and praise him. All this is "to the praise of his glory."

Prayer that God enlighten the Ephesians to see his gracious power

[15]For this reason, ever since I heard about your faith in the Lord Jesus and your love for all the saints, [16]I have not stopped giving thanks for you, remembering you in my prayers. [17]I keep asking that the God of our Lord Jesus Christ, the glorious Father, may give you the Spirit of wisdom and revelation, so that you may know him better. [18]I pray also that the eyes of your heart may be enlightened in order that you may know the hope to which he has called you, the riches of his glorious inheritance in the saints, [19]and his incomparably great power for us who believe. That power is like the working of his mighty strength, [20]which he exerted in Christ when he raised him from the dead and seated him at his right hand in the heavenly realms, [21]far above all rule and authority, power and dominion, and every title that can be given, not only in the present age but also in the one to come. [22]And God placed all things under his feet and appointed him to be head over everything for the church, [23]which is his body, the fullness of him who fills everything in every way.

Three times in the doxology just completed (verses 3-14) Paul urged the Ephesians to praise God for the great spiritual blessings they had received in the Father's electing them, the Son's redeeming them, and the Spirit's bringing them to faith and sealing their salvation. Recall that God did all this "to the praise of his glory."

In the spirit of praise and thanksgiving Paul now prays, "For this reason, ever since I heard about your faith in the Lord Jesus and your love for all the saints, I have not stopped giving thanks for you, remembering you in my prayers."

From the book of Acts we know that Paul served in Ephesus for three years. Because Paul here says "I *heard* about your faith," some have concluded that the letter could not have been intended for the Ephesians, because Paul would not speak that way to people whom he had served for three years. Note, however, that Paul had been in captivity in Rome for almost three years by the time he wrote this letter. Hence, it is entirely likely that Paul's best and most recent source of information about the readers was what he had *heard* via the reports that had come to him.

Be that as it may, it doesn't change Paul's model prayer of praise to God for the faith and love of his readers, for whom he prays constantly. Faith and love are not essentially different. Love is simply faith in action, and both are produced by the gospel, which alone can win hearts and lives for the Lord Jesus Christ.

Paul's prayer, however, is not restricted to praise. He adds a petition, or request, for the Ephesians. "I keep asking that the God of our Lord Jesus Christ, the glorious Father, may give you the Spirit of wisdom and revelation, so that you may know him better."

Only in and through Christ may sinful people approach God in prayer. Hence Paul addresses God as "the God of our Lord Jesus Christ, the glorious Father." He is not only Christ's Father, but by our faith in Christ he is also our Father. Hence we may come to him boldly and confidently, as "dear children coming to their dear Father." This is what Paul does when he asks the Father to give the Ephesians a gift, that is, "the Spirit of wisdom and revelation."

Spirit with a capital *S* would suggest that Paul is praying for the Holy Spirit to impart wisdom to the Ephesians. Such an understanding is certainly possible. But because Paul in the next verse prays that "the eyes of your heart may be enlightened," it is perhaps likelier that Paul is here asking God to give the Ephesians enlightened hearts and minds, which come from learning God's truths as they are revealed in his holy Word. Paul's prayer is that the Ephesians grow in their understanding of these truths so they may know God ever more fully.

For that increase in knowledge to happen, God must intervene. So Paul prays to God "that the eyes of your heart may be enlightened." Such enlightenment from the Word will help the Ephesians to recognize and appreciate three great blessings from the Father: (1) the hope to which he has called them, (2) the riches of his glorious inheritance in the saints, and (3) his incomparably great power for those who believe.

In speaking of the hope to which God has called the Ephesians, Paul is not using the word as when we say, "I hope to finish this job today" or "I hope it won't rain." The hope of which Paul speaks is not a fond wish, but a sure and certain confidence. It can be so because it rests on God's call. Recall that Paul reminded the Ephesians that from eternity God chose them, in time he redeemed them, and now he has sealed them by giving them his Holy Spirit.

While all this is sure and certain, it is, however, a promise for which full realization lies in the future. Hence Paul's further petition that the eyes of their hearts might be enlightened to see and comprehend "the riches of his glorious inheritance in the saints." An inheritance is not something earned or deserved. It's a gift; it's grace. And that's how God deals with his saints, that is, with the believers whom he has called, redeemed, and sealed with the Spirit.

But this hope and this inheritance both rest on a promise, and both lie in the future. Where, then, is the assurance that God can and will keep his promise? Paul prays that the eyes of their hearts may be enlightened so they might see God's "incomparably great power for us who believe." Knowing about God's power is the basis for trusting that God can and will keep his word.

But where's the proof of his power? Paul calls the Ephesians' attention to what God did in and through Christ. The apostle asserts, "That power is like the working of his mighty strength, which he exerted in Christ when he raised him from the dead and seated him at his right hand in the heavenly realms." For the believer an incomparably great power is at work, which is like the power God demonstrated in connection with the resurrection of his Son. Although Jesus always remained true God, even when he took on human flesh and became true man, he humbled himself and laid aside his divine power. He became obedient to his Father's will, even to death. There was no life in the corpse that Nicodemus and Joseph of Arimathea took down from the cross late on Good Friday afternoon. But God used his incomparably great power to restore his Son to life and give back what had originally been his. In addition to this, God greatly exalted him.

At the Ascension the Father welcomed his Son back to heaven and set the God-man at his right hand, giving him a position of power. In fact, he exalted him "far above all rule and authority, power and dominion, and every title that can be given." Paul uses four terms to describe positions of great power. He could no doubt have listed more than four, or he might have settled for fewer. The number of positions is not significant. The point is that absolutely no authority figure can successfully oppose the risen and ascended Christ. He is Lord over them all. And this is true not only for the present, but also for the future. Jesus is far above all opposition, "not only in the present age but also in the one to come."

To take Christ's exalted state one step farther, Paul states that he is not only above all authority figures, but he is in

141

charge of *everything* that happens. The apostle states, "God placed all things under his feet and appointed him to be head over everything for the church, which is his body, the fullness of him who fills everything in every way." Where is the assurance that God can and will keep his promise? Paul's answer is, The power that God has vested in his Son makes that absolutely certain, particularly when we see the favored relationship we have to this all-powerful Lord. God placed him over all persons of authority and put him in charge of absolutely everything "for the church, which is his body."

Christ's rule is absolute, and all his power is now used for one grand purpose, the good of his church, which consists of the sum total of all believers. The relationship between Christ and the rulers and authority figures is simply that of a lord and master dealing with subordinates. Christ's relationship with his church, however, is entirely different. It is an organic relationship, a connection as close as the one the head shares with the members of the body.

Paul is going to use this picture of head and body in yet another setting. Later in this letter he urges husbands to "love their wives as their own bodies. . . . After all, no one ever hated his own body, but he feeds and cares for it, *just as Christ does the church*" (5:28,29). In the present chapter Paul's point is that with the all-powerful Christ feeding and caring for us, we, the members of his church, can rest in complete security.

But Paul says yet another thing regarding Christ's relationship to the church. He calls the church "the fullness of him who fills everything in every way." That statement is actually something of a paradox, an apparent contradiction in terms. Christ fills everything in every way. He is completely self-sufficient. Yet he chooses to be empty and unfulfilled without his church. How can that be? Simply because God is true to

142

his eternal plan. From eternity he elected and predestined the members of his church—and he will not rest until he has accomplished their salvation. Only then will he be truly fulfilled. Paul prays the Ephesians and we may see this truth with enlightened eyes.

God's eternal plan of salvation was devised already in eternity, but it was carried out in time. To that aspect of the triune God's gracious dealing with us, Paul turns next.

God's eternal plan of salvation was carried out in time

Both Jews and Gentiles are saved by grace

It is important to keep in mind that the congregation in Ephesus was a mixed congregation made up of both Jews and Gentiles. How that came about becomes more apparent when we understand Paul's missionary methodology. In the book of Acts Luke tells us that whenever Paul came to a new area, he went first to the Jewish synagogue. There he proclaimed Jesus of Nazareth as the Christ, the fulfillment of God's Old Testament prophecies that promised the Jews a Savior.

Invariably this proclamation of Jesus of Nazareth as the promised Messiah drew a mixed reaction. A minority of Jews believed Paul's message and accepted Jesus as their Savior. The majority, however, refused Paul's message and forced Paul and his Christian converts to find a different place of worship. Thus a new Christian congregation formed with a nucleus of Jewish believers well versed in God's Word (that is, the Old Testament).

Numerical growth in the new congregation, however, came primarily from the Gentile neighbors and townspeople with whom the Jewish Christians shared their new-found Savior. These congregations soon became predominantly Gentile, but they retained strong leadership from the smaller

143

group of Jews who were well versed in Old Testament Scripture. This leadership proved to be particularly valuable when Paul moved on—often quite soon—to other areas of mission endeavor and left the new congregations on their own.

The point to be noted is that while the larger segment of the Ephesian congregation was probably of Gentile background, it also had a significant Jewish element. Paul addresses both Jews and Gentiles in his letter.

2 **As for you, you were dead in your transgressions and sins, ²in which you used to live when you followed the ways of this world and of the ruler of the kingdom of the air, the spirit who is now at work in those who are disobedient.**

When Paul says, "As for you," he is talking to the Ephesians of Gentile background. Their Jewish counterparts will be addressed later. For now Paul is speaking to Gentiles, and he has some very damaging things to say.

Although physically they were very much alive and active, Paul tells the Ephesians that spiritually they had been dead. Corpses can't move. Dead people can't do anything; they are totally unable to help themselves. Such was the spiritual plight in which the Gentile Ephesians had found themselves. If any were inclined to question Paul's diagnosis regarding their spiritual bankruptcy, he urged them to take a look at their lives and actions. That they had been dead in transgressions and sins is evident from the kind of lives they used to live when they "followed the ways of this world."

Like their friends and neighbors, the Ephesians had shown the common weaknesses and shortcomings of Gentile society. They had been godless and immoral, loveless, lazy, and disobedient. Society is that way, Paul says, because it follows "the ruler of the kingdom of the air, the spirit who is now at work in those who are disobedient." That "ruler," of course, is Satan (John 12:31; 14:30). He is a powerful and dangerous foe. Like a roaring lion he stalks about, seeking victims to devour (1 Peter 5:8). And the Ephesian Gentiles had been easy prey.

Paul's analysis did not apply only to them, though. Despite the Jews' considerable advantages in being God's chosen people, in their natural condition they were no better off than the Gentiles.

³All of us also lived among them at one time, gratifying the cravings of our sinful nature and following its desires and thoughts. Like the rest, we were by nature objects of wrath.

When Paul says, "We also lived among *them*," he includes himself and his fellow Jews with the disobedient Gentiles. True, Paul and the Jews may have disobeyed in a little different way, but in the final analysis they were just as guilty as the Gentiles. Paul had charged the Ephesian Gentiles with coarse and sinful *actions*. For himself and his fellow Jews Paul now admits to sinful *thoughts* and *desires*.

God's law, given to Israel on Mount Sinai, guided and regulated nearly every phase of Jewish life. As such, the law held in check among the Jews many of the coarse outbreaks of sin that were scandalously common among the Gentiles. But even this outward Jewish decency wasn't the full and complete obedience that a holy God rightly expects and deserves. Their very nature—hearts, minds, and attitudes— was tainted to the core. That showed itself in their "gratifying the cravings of [their] sinful nature and following its desires and thoughts." Like the Gentiles, Paul and his fellow Jews were by nature spiritually dead.

Whether they are open or secret, blatant or subtle, sinful actions and thoughts infect every man, woman, and child since the fall into sin. Sin is an inherited condition. We bring it with us from birth. And it rightly earns us the anger of a holy and just God. With Paul we too need to say, "Like the rest, we were by nature objects of wrath."

Paul paints a grim picture. All people are by nature spiritually dead, totally unable to change their condition. Not only are they unable to improve their lot, but they are the objects of an offended God's wrath. They can expect nothing but the harshest of punishment—and that for all eternity.

This would be a terrifying chapter if not for the fact that Paul can continue with a "but." That three-letter conjunction is the pivotal point of this chapter, yes, of the whole letter—in fact, of all Scripture. Mankind as a group has made a terrible mess of things. In their wickedness and perversity all people are at odds with God. All are spiritually dead and enemies of God. All deserve the severest punishment,

⁴But because of his great love for us, God, who is rich in mercy, ⁵made us alive with Christ even when we were dead in transgressions—it is by grace you have been saved.

These verses contain three enormously important words that give us a look into the heart and mind of our God. Paul can speak of a momentous change in our situation. Why? "Because of his [God's] great love for us." The Greek term for "love" used here is not the word that speaks of friendship between two people—people who see endearing qualities in each other and on that basis like each other. Instead, it speaks of a love and affection that is totally one-way. It all comes from God. Nothing in man the sinner, the God-hater, the spiritual corpse, drew God to him. Love resided only in the heart of God.

The second great term describing our Savior-God is "mercy." Paul speaks of him as "God, who is rich in mercy." Mercy is a positive quality that certainly has much in common with love. But it is also somewhat different. Mercy is the attitude in the mind and heart of God that moves him to take pity on us when he sees our lost and wretched state. Mercy prompts him to action.

And what did God's love and mercy prompt him to do? We were rightly the objects of divine wrath, "but because of his great love for us, God, who is rich in mercy, made us alive with Christ even when we were dead in transgressions."

Paul has already told us about the incomparably great power God used to raise Christ from the dead. But that use of God's power in raising Christ has far-reaching implications also for the whole human race. Raising Christ from physical death signaled the completion of Christ's saving work and sealed our redemption. It made possible our resurrection from spiritual death.

When Paul says, "God . . . made us alive with Christ," he is referring to the miracle of conversion. When we could not lift a finger to help ourselves, God through Word and sacrament worked faith in our hearts, creating life where formerly there had been none. In this way he "made us alive with Christ even when we were dead in transgressions."

God's love and mercy in action, converting and making spiritually dead people alive, is such a marvelous and amazing thing that Paul spontaneously exclaims, "It is by grace you have been saved." Together with love and mercy, "grace" is the third term that requires our attention. But actually, Paul is getting a little ahead of himself. He'll treat the concept of grace more fully beginning at verse 8. First he continues to explain what God's love and mercy have done for us.

⁶And God raised us up with Christ and seated us with him in the heavenly realms in Christ Jesus, ⁷in order that in the com-

147

ing ages he might show the incomparable riches of his grace, expressed in his kindness to us in Christ Jesus.

Paul sketches the whole cycle of the Christian's life: past, present, and future. In the past the Ephesians—and Paul too—were spiritually dead, as shown by the Ephesians' evil deeds and Paul's evil thoughts and desires. But now, having been brought to faith in Christ, they are spiritually alive. That opens up grand new possibilities. In a manner of speaking, Christians already have everything. Even now in their lives of faith they are as good as in heaven with Christ. Recall Paul's bold statement at the close of the first chapter: "God placed all things under his [Christ's] feet and appointed him to be head over everything for the church, which is his body." Christ has all power on earth and in heaven, and he uses it all for the benefit of his believers. This is why Paul can say that even while living here on earth, they have been raised with Christ and are actually seated with him in heaven.

The full realization of the bliss of heaven is, of course, still in the future. But God did not make us alive just to give us a small foretaste of heaven. He did so "in order that in the coming ages he might show the incomparable riches of his grace, expressed in his kindness to us in Christ Jesus." As great and glorious as God's present blessings to us are, they don't begin to compare with what God will do for his believers in heaven. Scripture tries to help us form some concept of heaven. For example, it refers to life in heaven as a gala wedding banquet, or it compares heaven to a glorious city paved with gold and set with precious gemstones. All those pictures, however, fall short of the real thing—as they must, of course—because what God has in store for us is "incomparable" by Paul's definition. There simply is nothing in our present range of experience that can compare with heaven, so

148

great is the love and mercy of our God, "expressed in his kindness to us in Christ Jesus."

After holding before the Ephesians' eyes the present good fortune they already enjoy and the even greater riches they by faith may confidently anticipate in heaven, Paul returns once more to the source and cause of all this blessedness.

⁸For it is by grace you have been saved, through faith—and this not from yourselves, it is the gift of God—⁹not by works, so that no one can boast.

After outlining for us what God's love and mercy have done, Paul now gives center stage to the concept of grace. Like love and mercy, *grace* is a term that gives us a glimpse into the heart and mind of God. The essential aspect of God's grace is that it speaks of a quality in God that makes him willing—yes, even eager—to give us undeserving sinners great and precious gifts. Substitute "undeserved gift" for the term "grace" and you catch the sense of what Paul is telling the Ephesians: "It is an *undeserved gift* that through faith you have been saved, for God gave you saving faith as a gift."

By definition, faith is trust and confidence that takes God at his word. But recall that both Jews and Gentiles—which is to say, all people—are by nature dead in transgressions and sins. They can't bring themselves to faith; they can't decide to trust God's promises and accept Christ as their Savior. Paul nails this important truth down with three unmistakably clear statements. He tells the Ephesians their conversion is (1) not from themselves; (2) the gift of God; (3) not by works. With two negatives and a positive Paul leaves absolutely no doubt that the sinner's conversion is God's doing, not man's. As a result, "no one can boast" as though he had done something to save himself or that his works in any way contributed to his salvation. Salvation is by grace, an unde-

*"For it is by grace you have been saved,
through faith." (2:8)*

served gift freely given by God without the contribution of any human works.

A life of good works is, however, what God has in mind for every Christian. It is a part of that creative, life-giving process that God set in motion when in his kindness he called us to faith in his Son. Paul indicates the place of works when he says,

[10]For we are God's workmanship, created in Christ Jesus to do good works, which God prepared in advance for us to do.

With our new God-given spiritual life we are indeed able to respond to God's will. We are able, albeit imperfectly, to do what God wants. It is not that we *have* to, but rather that we *want* to do God's will. The good works that flow from faith are simply an opportunity to show our appreciation for all that God in Christ has done for us. It would be hard to improve on the apostle John's terse analysis: "We love [God] because he first loved us" (1 John 4:19).

But even the good deeds we do are no basis for boasting. They're really not our own doing; we're simply being given the opportunity to do the good things "which God prepared in advance for us to do."

Paul has certainly made his point: Our salvation is totally and completely the gift of a gracious God. We did nothing, and we have no grounds for boasting.

Jews and Gentiles are united into one church

In the opening section of this chapter Paul reminded the Gentile Ephesians of their sorry and disgraceful past. But all that has changed, now that they have found Christ—or rather, now that Christ has found them.

However, another change has taken place, a change on a much larger scale. A new era has dawned with the coming of

Christ. Though Paul does not use the terms, he is, in fact, inviting the Ephesians to see what grand possibilities have opened up now that the *Old Testament* has been completed and the *New Testament* has begun.

The barriers and hedges God set around Israel in the form of rules and regulations, intended to keep them a separate nation, have now served their purpose. The division between Jews and Gentiles has become an anachronism, an outdated and unnecessary complication. As one organic unit, the Christian church now enfolds and unites all believers in Christ. Paul invites the Ephesians to see and to appreciate the change by comparing their former state with what they have now become.

¹¹Therefore, remember that formerly you who are Gentiles by birth and called "uncircumcised" by those who call themselves "the circumcision" (that done in the body by the hands of men)—¹²remember that at that time you were separate from Christ, excluded from citizenship in Israel and foreigners to the covenants of the promise, without hope and without God in the world.

Accepting circumcision was the sign and seal by which a Jewish male indicated his willingness to live under God's covenant. Circumcision denoted him as a "son of the covenant," one of God's chosen people. Claiming this favored status for themselves made it very easy for Jews to look down on the less-favored Gentiles. Referring to a Gentile as "uncircumcised" was a term of reproach, the equivalent of calling him an outcast and a reprobate sinner.

Paul certainly is not approving of the animosity and bias that underlay many of the derisive terms the Jews heaped on the Gentiles. But he does acknowledge a basis for the standard Jewish opinions regarding Gentiles and the Jews' low esteem of the Gentiles' spiritual status. They were right in thinking that the Gentiles in general were lost.

To see how true this was, Paul's Gentile readers in Ephesus need merely to think back on their miserable condition prior to the days when Paul came to them with the gospel. "Remember that at that time you were separate from Christ," Paul says. That was a terrible problem, an insurmountable obstacle. And Paul reinforces how desperate their situation was by adding four more negative descriptors. The Gentiles were

> excluded from citizenship in Israel,
> foreigners to the covenants of the promise,
> without hope, and
> without God in the world.

Recall that at Jacob's well Jesus told the Samaritan woman, "Salvation is from the Jews" (John 4:22). For Gentiles to be "excluded from citizenship in Israel" and "foreigners to the covenants" that promised the Messiah was a dreadful plight. It made their situation hopeless. Paul can rightly say they were "without hope" because they were "without God in the world." It is not that they were atheists who denied the existence of a god. They had many gods, but they were false gods. They did not have the triune God, so they had no god at all to help them.

Paul doesn't dredge up these old memories to hurt the Ephesians but to help them, not to pull them down but to build them up. He wants them to make a comparison. Formerly they were without hope and without God in the world, but all that has changed.

¹³But now in Christ Jesus you who once were far away have been brought near through the blood of Christ.

Formerly they were "separate from Christ," but now they are "in Christ Jesus." Formerly they were "far away" from the covenant and God's promised salvation, but now they "have been brought near." Note that the verb in the last sentence is passive. The Gentiles did not do anything on their own to approach God. They "were brought" near. It was all God's doing—and it cost him a tremendous price. That change could come about only "through the blood of Christ." "In Christ" the Gentiles, formerly outsiders, now have been brought into God's church. Hence, a whole new age has dawned. Again, Paul does not use the term *New Testament*, but that is really what he is talking about.

In the next paragraph the apostle enlarges on this world-changing event by dividing it into three component parts. His thought progression can perhaps best be sketched with three sets of questions and answers:

1. How did God accomplish the change from the Old Testament to the New Testament? *Answer:* by sending Christ, thereby destroying the dividing wall of hostility (verses 14,15a).
2. Why did God do it? *Answer:* to create one new man out of the two (verses 15b,16).
3. What are the results of God's work in Christ? *Answer:* peace between Jew and Gentile, with free access to the Father for both (verses 17,18).

How did God accomplish the change from the Old Testament to the New Testament?

¹⁴For he himself is our peace, who has made the two one and has destroyed the barrier, the dividing wall of hostility, ¹⁵by abolishing in his flesh the law with its commandments and regulations.

When Paul here speaks of the "law," it is important to recognize what he's referring to. God gave Israel a threefold law: civil, ceremonial, and moral. The moral law, summarized in the Ten Commandments, expresses God's holy and unchangeable will for all people of all time. As such, it was not only binding on Israel but also on the Gentiles. It was wrong for both to worship idols, kill, steal, or covet.

However, the civil law (dealing with God's governance of Israel) and the ceremonial laws (such as dietary prescriptions for clean and unclean food) were restrictions binding only on Israel. For example, Gentiles were not forbidden to eat pork.

The purpose of these civil and ceremonial laws, unique to Israel, was to keep Israel a separate nation. The many carefully spelled out regulations were to hedge and protect Israel from heathen influence until the promised Messiah was born.

These rules and regulations, so useful for keeping Jews and Gentiles apart, also bred a great deal of ill will and hatred between the two. Thus the civil and ceremonial laws became a "dividing wall of hostility."

The need to keep Israel a separate nation ended when Jesus was born in Bethlehem. The civil and ceremonial laws had fulfilled their purpose. When Jesus on the cross declared, "It is finished," he was speaking of the completion of our salvation, but his words also marked the end of the Old Testament and its rules and regulations. "In his flesh" Christ on the cross abolished "the law with its commandments and regulations."

Why did God do it?

His purpose was to create in himself one new man out of the two, thus making peace, ¹⁶and in this one body to reconcile both of them to God through the cross, by which he put to death their hostility.

Christ's cross put an end to the binding force of the Old Testament civil and ceremonial laws, thus removing the dividing wall of hostility between Jew and Gentile. The removal of this dividing wall between these two groups of people was only part of Christ's work, however. The real problem was not between Jew and Gentile but between both groups of people and God. Consequently, the far greater accomplishment of Christ's cross was that his blood paid for the sins of the whole world. Christ's perfect life and innocent death earned the merit that avails before God. It secured the sinner's release from the guilt of his sins.

Paul calls his readers' attention to the fact that when God reconciled both Jews and Gentiles to himself, he also laid the foundation for their reconciliation to each other. That reconciliation also was in Christ's heart and mind, for "his purpose was to create in himself one new man out of the two." Out of the "two," that is, Jew and Gentile, Christ purposed to create "one man," that is, one organic unit, the holy Christian church. This Christian church is a new creation, a thought that will engage Paul at some length later in this letter.

For now, he speaks of the results of Christ's work. Those results will become clearer to the Ephesians when they remember their own good fortune in being found by God's grace and being brought into his fold, the church.

What are the results of God's work in Christ?

¹⁷He came and preached peace to you who were far away and peace to those who were near. ¹⁸For through him we both have access to the Father by one Spirit.

Christ not only redeemed sinners from the guilt and punishment of their sins, but he also made sure the good news of his victory over sin and death was proclaimed. "He came and preached peace to you," Paul states. It was Paul, of course, who came to the Ephesians, but he was not his own man. He was merely an ambassador, a representative who "became a servant of this gospel by the gift of God's grace" (3:7). It was really Christ who spoke to the Ephesians—through his called public servants. Hence the apostle can say that Christ came and preached to them.

The good news he brought was twofold. First, Christ brought peace—"peace to you who were far away [Gentiles] and peace to those who were near [Jews]." It bears repeating that the basis for peace is Christ's redemptive work on the cross. Not only does that reconcile the sinner to God, it also forms the basis for a reconciliation between sinners, thus forging a complete, true, and lasting peace.

A second gift that comes through Christ's preaching of reconciliation is the realization that an equality exists between forgiven sinners. Paul alludes to that when he continues, "For through him [Christ] we both have access to the Father by one Spirit." Jewish and Gentile believers stand on the same plane. Both may come directly to the Father with their prayers and petitions.

Recall that the status of Jew and Gentile before God became a matter of debate in Galatia, where Judaizers were causing problems for the congregations there. Judaizers were Jewish Christians who acknowledged the need for faith in Christ. Unfortunately, they were of the opinion that faith by itself was not enough for salvation. They claimed that Gentile converts also needed to observe the Old Testament ceremonial rules and regulations. In effect, they said that Gentile converts had to come to God through Judaism, that is, they had to become proselytes.

In his letter to the Galatians Paul strongly opposed that view, asserting that salvation is by faith alone, without the addition of any human works or actions. To the Galatians Paul wrote, "You are all sons of God through faith in Christ Jesus, for all of you who were baptized into Christ have clothed yourselves with Christ. There is neither Jew nor Greek, slave nor free, male nor female, for you are all one in Christ Jesus" (Galatians 3:26-28). Paul says the same thing here to the Ephesians, "Through him [Christ] we both [Jews and Gentiles] have access to the Father by one Spirit."

That insight has major implications for the relationship of Jews and Gentiles to one another in the Christian church. And the church, you will recall, is the central theme of Paul's letter to the Ephesians.

[19]Consequently, you are no longer foreigners and aliens, but fellow citizens with God's people and members of God's household, [20]built on the foundation of the apostles and prophets, with Christ Jesus himself as the chief cornerstone. [21]In him the whole building is joined together and rises to become a holy temple in the Lord. [22]And in him you too are being built together to become a dwelling in which God lives by his Spirit.

By faith in Christ the Gentile Christians in Ephesus and Gentile believers in general have the same access to God as God's covenant people enjoyed all along. This allows Paul to draw a conclusion. He opens this section with the introductory word "consequently." It is as if he were saying: Since you Ephesians have the same direct access to God as the covenant people always had, it follows that "you are no longer foreigners and aliens, but fellow citizens with God's people and members of God's household."

Recall that formerly when the Ephesian Gentiles were without Christ they were "excluded from citizenship in Israel and foreigners to the covenants of the promise" (verse 12). By faith in Christ all that has changed. Now they no longer lack a place in the kingdom of God. Now they are fellow citizens with God's people.

They are not only citizens of the same kingdom, but they are even closer than that. They are members of the same family. God is, after all, their Father, and they have access to him just as the Jewish believers do.

So far Paul has tried to help his readers picture the close relationship in the church between Gentile Christians and Jewish believers by directing their attention to such concepts as citizenship in a kingdom or membership in the same family. Now he switches to the picture of a building and has them think of the unity and coherence between the various structural members of a building: the foundation, the cornerstone, the walls rising to form the superstructure. He says the Ephesians are "built on the foundation of the apostles and prophets, with Christ Jesus himself as the chief cornerstone."

The firm foundation of the Ephesian congregation, Paul states, is the doctrine Christ gave them through his Old Testament prophets and New Testament apostles. Throughout the ages there has been only one plan of salvation. Old Testament believers looked forward to the Messiah or Savior who was to come. New Testament believers look back to the Savior who has come. Hence the apostles and prophets, bearers of God's Word about the Savior, can fairly be called the "foundation" of the Ephesian congregation, and the Christ they preached its cornerstone.

But what is occurring in Ephesus is but one small example of what is going on all over the world wherever the gospel is preached. "In him [Christ]" the Apostle declares, "the whole building is joined together and rises to become a holy temple in the Lord." The "temple" to which Paul is referring is the holy Christian church. It is the sum total of all believers, those who in past ages waited in faith for the Messiah to

159

come and those who in the present trust in the merits of the Savior who has come. As the gospel progresses through the world, new believers are added daily to this church.

As carpenters and craftsmen add more and more component parts to a building as it proceeds toward completion, so too Christ is building his church—one believer at a time. Each believer is carefully fitted into his or her niche. All are known by name. All are important to the Builder. All fulfill a purpose. (Recall the "good works, which God prepared in advance for us to do" in verse 10). Hence, Paul can give his readers this assurance: "In him [Christ] you too are being built together to become a dwelling in which God lives by his Spirit."

God's eternal plan of salvation was preached to Gentiles by Paul

The "mystery" of God's grace revealed

3 **For this reason I, Paul, the prisoner of Christ Jesus for the sake of you Gentiles—**

When Paul says, "For this reason," he is referring to the central thought developed in chapter 2, namely, the unity in Christ that brings Jews and Gentiles together into one church. He is intending to ask God to enlighten the Ephesians, to bring them to understand ever more fully just how great Christ's love for them actually is. Paul's prayer will end with the request that God enable the Ephesians "to grasp how wide and long and high and deep is the love of Christ" (verse 18).

In this verse (3:1), which forms the introduction to his prayer, Paul refers to himself as "the prisoner of Christ Jesus for the sake of you Gentiles." Recall that this letter to the Ephesians was written while Paul was detained in Rome, awaiting trial for his Christian activity. He speaks of himself as imprisoned "for the sake of you Gentiles." That expression requires a bit more explanation, so before he begins his prayer, he digresses to show just how his ministry to Gentiles fits in with God's eternal plan.

²Surely you have heard about the administration of God's grace that was given to me for you, ³that is, the mystery made known to me by revelation, as I have already written briefly. ⁴In reading this, then, you will be able to understand my insight into the mystery of Christ, ⁵which was not made known to men in other generations as it has now been revealed by the Spirit to God's holy apostles and prophets. ⁶This mystery is that through the gospel the Gentiles are heirs together with Israel, members together of one body, and sharers together in the promise in Christ Jesus.

The NIV translation of verse 2 adequately reproduces what the original says but makes it easy to miss the emphasis Paul intended. The key point lies in the last two words, "for you." We might paraphrase the verse, Surely you have heard that it was *for your benefit*, not mine, that God called me to administer his grace. To be sure, Paul's faithful preaching of God's grace to Gentiles got him into trouble with his fellow Jews and put him on trial in the Roman legal system. In the final analysis, though, the office of administering God's grace to Gentiles wasn't something Paul chose for himself. It "was given to me," he declares. And so was the message.

Paul would never have figured out his message by himself. Rather, it was a "mystery made known to [him] by revelation." The term "mystery" is used some 20 times in the New Testament—most often by Paul and usually in the sense illustrated here. Paul is not speaking of something that is mysterious in the sense of being vague, murky, or hard to understand but rather something that needs to be explained. After it has

161

been explained, it's perfectly clear, but one would never have tumbled onto it without some outside help. Paul indicates that he received such help from God by revelation.

What was the "mystery" that was explained to Paul? In verse 6 Paul says, "This mystery is that through the gospel the Gentiles are heirs together with Israel, members together of one body, and sharers together in the promise in Christ Jesus."

The key to the mystery revealed to Paul lies in the expression "together," used three times. Actually, in the original Greek the "together" idea is found in the noun. One could reflect that by using English compound words with *co-*. Paul was given to understand that through faith in Christ Gentiles are *co-heirs* with believing Jews, *co-members* of one and the same body, that is, the church, and *co-sharers* with Israel in the salvation that Christ's merit has won. This equality between Jews and Gentiles is parallel to what Paul previously talked about when he stated that Christ's saving purpose in reconciling the world was "to create in himself one new man out of the two" (2:15). Paul seems to allude to his treatment of this subject earlier in the letter when he says, "As I have already written briefly." Urging them to go back to that section, Paul explains, "In reading this, then, you will be able to understand my insight into the mystery of Christ, which was not made known to men in other generations as it has now been revealed by the Spirit to God's holy apostles and prophets."

A word of caution is in order so that we don't misunderstand Paul's words and jump to the conclusion that Gentiles couldn't be saved or that God wasn't interested in them during Old Testament times. Recall that God through the Old Testament prophet Ezekiel said, "As surely as I live, declares the Sovereign LORD, I take no pleasure in

162

the death of the wicked, but rather that they turn from their ways and live" (33:11). These words applied to Gentiles as well as Jews.

That being the case, however, Paul can still say that the mystery of Christ "was not made known to men in other generations *as it has now been revealed* by the Spirit to God's holy apostles and prophets." Without using the term *New Testament,* in effect Paul is saying: We are in a new era now that the Old Testament prophecies have been fulfilled and the Messiah has come. In this new order, the gospel is being proclaimed not only to Jews but to Gentiles as well. This is illustrated by the call God graciously gave me.

The mystery proclaimed by Paul

Paul's call

⁷I became a servant of this gospel by the gift of God's grace given me through the working of his power. ⁸Although I am less than the least of all God's people, this grace was given me: to preach to the Gentiles the unsearchable riches of Christ, ⁹and to make plain to everyone the administration of this mystery, which for ages past was kept hidden in God, who created all things.

Paul says, "I *became* a servant of this gospel." He wasn't one originally. Paul always remained painfully aware that earlier in his career as an ardent Pharisee he had been violently opposed to Christ and a vicious persecutor of Christians. On one occasion, while on his way to Damascus to conduct a raid on Christians in that city, the risen Christ confronted Paul on the road. He literally knocked him to the ground and brusquely rebuked him, "Saul, Saul, why do you persecute me?" (Acts 9:4; see 9:1-19; 22:6-16; 26:12-18 for Paul's description of his call.)

Through the "working of his [Christ's] power" Paul became a convert to Christianity, a "servant of this gospel" who willingly accepted the assignment to carry the message of Christ to the Gentiles. This task certainly wasn't anything Paul sought or deserved. It was a gift. We have previously noted that the word *grace* can often be replaced with the term *undeserved gift*. Note how neatly that fits here. Although he is "less than the least of all God's people," Paul gratefully acknowledges that "this grace [undeserved gift] was given me: to preach to the Gentiles the unsearchable riches of Christ, and to make plain to everyone the administration of this mystery, which for ages past was kept hidden in God, who created all things."

The two infinitives (to preach, to make plain) do not refer to separate or different things, but together they explain and define what Paul's undeserved gift was. He was privileged to make plain what hadn't been clear before, namely, the place of Gentiles in God's plan. By revelation Paul received information that for ages past was kept hidden in God, who created all things. Now the "mystery" of equality between Jews and Gentiles in one church was revealed.

God's purpose

[10]His intent was that now, through the church, the manifold wisdom of God should be made known to the rulers and authorities in the heavenly realms, [11]according to his eternal purpose which he accomplished in Christ Jesus our Lord.

As Creator, God reserved the right to reveal this information to his creatures at precisely the best time. Paul gives us a glimpse of God's rationale for revealing the mystery. From eternity God had a plan of salvation to rescue fallen mankind. Recall that in chapter 1 of this letter Paul assured the Ephesians, "For he [God] chose us in him [Christ] before the creation of the world" (verse 4). God always intended to send his Son as the Savior, to be born as true man so he could be our Substitute.

To put this plan into action God in his wisdom chose Abraham from among all the families of the earth and made him the father of the Jewish nation. He gave this nation a special land, struck his covenant with them, kept them separate from the other nations, and gave them special rules and regulations. All this was to keep them a separate people until "the time had fully come" (Galatians 4:4) for the promised Savior to be born in the person of Jesus of Nazareth.

After Jesus' perfect life on earth and his innocent death on the cross, God raised his Son from death and received him back to heaven at the Ascension. Thus in Christ Jesus, God accomplished his eternal purpose of redeeming all people, Gentiles as well as Jews.

God's intention was for the Christian church to embrace all the redeemed—people "from every tribe and language and people and nation," as he inspired the apostle John to write in Revelation (5:9). But becoming such a world church involved a number of stages. The church born in Jerusalem on Pentecost was largely a Jewish Christian church. True, there were people in attendance from many lands (Acts 2:5-11), but they were predominantly people of Jewish background who had returned to Jerusalem for one of the annual pilgrim festivals.

The first influx into the Christian church of people other than Jews is recorded for us in Acts chapter 8, where we are told that Philip "went down to a city in Samaria and proclaimed the Christ there" (verse 5). Recall that Samaritans were the mixed race that developed in Palestine after the majority of Israelites were carried off into captivity. The very few Jews left in the Promised Land after the deportation intermarried with the displaced persons whom the conquerors brought in to inhabit the vacant land. Thus a mixed race resulted, which the Jews never acknowledged as kinsmen despite the fact that they had some Jewish genes. By a generous estimate Samaritans might be called half-Jews.

At any rate, by a visible display of the Holy Spirit, comparable to what happened in Jerusalem on Pentecost, God indicated that by virtue of their faith in Christ these half-Jewish Samaritans were welcome in the Christian church (Acts 8:14-17).

It remained for Cornelius, a Roman centurion and a full Gentile, to be the test case whereby the Holy Spirit indicated that God accepted into the church people who were not Jewish at all. It wasn't an easy lesson to learn. Even after receiving the vision of the great sheet let down from heaven containing both clean and unclean animals that Peter was told to eat (Acts 10:9-16), the apostle had misgivings about entering the Gentile home of Cornelius. But here too, when Cornelius and his household responded in faith to the message of Christ that Peter proclaimed, the Holy Spirit came upon these Gentiles (verses 44-48).

Still, doing mission work in earnest among the Gentiles lagged for a while. Luke reports: "Now those who had been scattered by the persecution in connection with Stephen traveled as far as Phoenicia, Cyprus and Antioch, telling the message only to Jews. Some of them, however, men from Cyprus and Cyrene, went to Antioch and began to speak to Greeks also, telling them the good news about the Lord Jesus. The Lord's hand was with them, and a great number of people believed and turned to the Lord" (Acts 11:19-21).

It was in Antioch of Syria, however, that work among the Gentiles really took off, particularly after Paul arrived on the scene. Again Luke is very helpful: "Barnabas went to Tarsus to look for Saul, and when he found him, he brought him to Antioch. So for a whole year Barnabas and Saul met with the church and taught great numbers of people. The disciples were called Christians first at Antioch" (Acts 11:25,26).

All this was in preparation for when God would formally send out Paul as his missionary to the Gentiles. Luke records the commissioning of Paul and Barnabas for this work in the opening verses of Acts 13. Paul has this commissioning as a missionary in mind when he writes to the Ephesians about the undeserved gift that was given him: to preach to the Gentiles the unsearchable riches of Christ.

Although preparing the means for bringing in Gentiles took some time, Paul tells the Ephesians that God's plan was perfectly on schedule. "His intent was that now, through the church, the manifold wisdom of God should be made known to the rulers and authorities in the heavenly realms."

God revealed the mystery of equality between Jewish and Gentile believers to Paul so that now, by the apostle's proclamation of the gospel, the Christian church might grow and flourish. Thus in the growth of the church, the good and gracious purpose of God to save sinners would become known to all people.

But not only people would come to know his plan. God would make it known even to "the rulers and authorities in the heavenly realms." In chapter 1 Paul listed four titles or categories of spiritual powers: rule, authority, power, and dominion (verse 21). There he was speaking of all spiritual powers, the bad as well as the good. Here Paul seems to have reduced his scope to just the good spiritual powers, that is, angels. They too are genuinely interested in the spread of the gospel and the growth of the church, as Peter indicated when he said, "Even angels long to look into these things" (1 Peter 1:12).

167

God's plan for the church is perfectly on track, and it brings the greatest of blessings. Not the least of these blessings is free access to the Father.

The believer's blessings

¹²In him and through faith in him we may approach God with freedom and confidence. ¹³I ask you, therefore, not to be discouraged because of my sufferings for you, which are your glory.

When Paul says "we," he is including himself (a Jew) with the Ephesian Gentiles. For both groups the barriers have been taken away in Christ—barriers between one another, but even more important, barriers between the sinner and God. Hence, both groups now have free access to God. No preliminary sacrifices are required; there is no need for a priest or intercessor. Both Jew and Gentile may come directly to God. Not only do they have the *freedom* to come to God, but they have the joy and pleasure of coming *confidently*, without any reservation, "as dear children coming to their dear father."

Not even Paul's imprisonment can hamper their joyous confidence that God is in charge. Paul's imprisonment is not a setback but part of God's plan to further the growth of the church. It will bring into even sharper focus the "glory" the Gentiles now enjoy by virtue of their fortunate state in God's overall plan. (For a later statement from Paul that this confidence regarding his current imprisonment was not misplaced, see Philippians 1:12-14.)

Prayer that God enable the Ephesians to comprehend the love of Christ

¹⁴For this reason I kneel before the Father, ¹⁵from whom his whole family in heaven and on earth derives its name. ¹⁶I pray

that out of his glorious riches he may strengthen you with power through his Spirit in your inner being, [17]so that Christ may dwell in your hearts through faith. And I pray that you, being rooted and established in love, [18]may have power, together with all the saints, to grasp how wide and long and high and deep is the love of Christ, [19]and to know this love that surpasses knowledge—that you may be filled to the measure of all the fullness of God.

You may recall that Paul opened this chapter with what we described as the *introduction* to a prayer. Before getting into the prayer, Paul digressed to explain the mystery that God had revealed to him, that in the Christian church God is pleased to have Jewish and Gentile believers in Christ stand as equals. God's undeserved gift to Paul was choosing him to be the revealer of this mystery, sending him out as the bearer of this good news, particularly to Gentiles.

So that Gentiles in general and his Ephesian readers in particular might understand the true greatness of what God in Christ had done for them, Paul once more returns to his prayer for their enlightenment.

This prayer consists essentially of three petitions followed by a doxology, a statement of praise to God. Paul asks God to grant the Ephesians strength, knowledge, and fullness.

These, however, are not three isolated or separate things. They all hang together. We could connect and expand them a bit by putting them together into one sentence, such as, Paul prays that God would *strengthen* the new man in the Ephesians, in order that they would come to *know* the greatness of Christ's love and so gain a deeper realization of the *fullness* that is theirs as members of God's family.

Petition for strength

In Christ, God is the Father of all believers. Hence believers of all time are united into one family, the holy Christian church. That family includes glorified believers already in heaven as well as those still living on earth.

As a member of this great family, Paul comes boldly to God as his heavenly Father. On this occasion his prayer is for other family members, specifically the Ephesians. In humble reverence Paul kneels "before the Father, from whom his whole family in heaven and on earth derives its name" and makes his intercession. He says, "I pray that out of his glorious riches he [God] may strengthen you with power through his Spirit in your inner being, so that Christ may dwell in your hearts through faith."

Paul requests that God would give the Ephesians strength—*spiritual* strength, which comes only through the Holy Spirit. The Spirit's work affects the "inner being," that is, the new man created when the Ephesians were brought to faith. This new man grows as the Spirit continues to work in believers through Word and sacrament, making them ever more sure and confident of their salvation as faith in Christ grows.

Causing Christ to dwell in believers' hearts is the real work of the Holy Spirit. It is important to keep that in mind in an age when people who speak of charismatic gifts of the Spirit are likely to be thinking of speaking in tongues or bringing about healings as though that were the true work of the Spirit.

Recall what Christ on Maundy Thursday evening said about the Holy Spirit's work: "When the Counselor comes, whom I will send to you from the Father, the Spirit of truth who goes out from the Father, *he will testify about me*" (John 15:26). The Spirit's main work is advancing Christ: bringing people to faith in Christ and then strengthening that faith. So Paul asks God to send his Holy Spirit to do his strengthening work in the hearts of the Ephesians "so that Christ may dwell in your hearts through faith."

Petition for knowledge

Paul's second petition for the Ephesians is that, being mightily strengthened by the Spirit in their new man, they would be able to comprehend the greatness of Christ's love for them. Hence he continues, "And I pray that you, being rooted and established in love, may have power, together with all the saints, to grasp how wide and long and high and deep is the love of Christ, and to know this love that surpasses knowledge."

Paul is praying for people who have been "rooted and established in love." "Rooted" involves the picture of a plant, alive and vibrant, poised to grow. "Established" suggests a different picture. Literally it means "founded upon" or "based on a foundation." What the Ephesians are rooted in and based upon is the love that Christ has shown for them.

Paul asks the Ephesians to stop and think of Christ's amazing love. When they were dead in transgressions and sins (2:1), God sent his Son to suffer and die for them. In this way he made them alive and by faith brought them into his church.

The Ephesians experienced that marvelous love in their own lives, but they had only begun to learn about it. Paul now prays that God would enable them to grasp or understand the full extent of Christ's love. Paul suggests that the Ephesians think of how Christ's love stretches out in all directions (width, length, height, depth) to embrace "all the saints," that is, every believer who ever lived. For each believer of all time, in every place, Christ has done exactly the same as he did for the Ephesians, so great is his love for so many people who were so worthless and unworthy of being saved! God in Christ reached out to them all and brought them into the great temple he is building, the holy Christian church (2:21).

Paul admits that to fully comprehend the love God has shown to and through the church really "surpasses knowledge," but he prays that the Ephesians would at least start grasping the greatness of Christ's love.

Petition for fullness

Paul, however, does not pray just for abstract knowledge and understanding on the Ephesians' part. He wants them to participate fully in God's good gifts. Hence he continues: I pray "that you may be filled to the measure of all the fullness of God."

God, of course, has total "fullness." He created everything; he owns everything; he controls everything. And yet, he allows us, his dear children, to come boldly to him. In fact, he invites us to pray confidently, assuring us that he will hear. Paul's prayer is a model of bold prayer. There's nothing bashful about his request. He doesn't ask for just a few crumbs; he asks for the whole loaf. His request is that the Ephesians "may be filled to the measure of all the fullness of God." We might say that he is asking that the Ephesians be filled to overflowing with all the good things that God dispenses through his church.

Doxology

[20]Now to him who is able to do immeasurably more than all we ask or imagine, according to his power that is at work within us, [21]to him be glory in the church and in Christ Jesus throughout all generations, for ever and ever! Amen.

It is significant that Paul again calls the Ephesians' attention to the personal experience they have had with God's power. That great power brought them to faith and made them members of Christ's church. It is like the power God used to raise Christ from the dead (1:19,20).

On the basis of the mighty deeds God has already done, Paul can confidently call upon him as one "who is able to do immeasurably more than all we ask or imagine." With God nothing is impossible. Hence we can never ask too much of him. Since we have such a God, well might we also join Paul's doxology and say, "To him be glory in the church and in Christ Jesus throughout all generations, for ever and ever!" Paul punctuates his prayer with an "amen." That is to say: "This is most certainly true. This is going to happen."

We noted that verses 14 to 21 are set as an intercessory prayer; Paul prayed for the Ephesians. But Christians have for centuries prayed this also for themselves. Let us change it to first person and see how fitting and appropriate it becomes as a prayer for each of us to pray individually.

> For this reason I kneel before the Father, from whom his whole family in heaven and on earth derives its name. I pray that out of his glorious riches he may strengthen me with power through his Spirit in my inner being, so that Christ may dwell in my heart through faith. And I pray that, being rooted and established in love, I may have power, together with all the saints, to grasp how wide and long and high and deep is the love of Christ, and to know this love that surpasses knowledge—that I may be filled to the measure of all the fullness of God.

> Now to him who is able to do immeasurably more than all I ask or imagine, according to his

power that is at work within me, to him be glory in the church and in Christ Jesus throughout all generations, for ever and ever! Amen.

PART TWO
THE BLESSED EFFECTS
OF GOD'S SAVING GRACE
(EPHESIANS 4:1–6:20)

Paul's letters tend to divide into two fairly equal parts: the first half of the letter being a doctrinal portion and the second half a "practical" section. "Practical" is to be understood in the sense of an application of the doctrine to the everyday life of the reader.

This pattern can be observed also in the letter to the Ephesians. The first three chapters have dealt with the great things God has done for us in Christ. Through Christ's redemptive work the Christian church was established. In that church both Jews and Gentiles, by God's amazing grace, are welcome as equals and "are being built together to become a dwelling in which God lives by his Spirit" (2:22). The concluding three chapters deal, then, with the Christian's response to God's grace. How does God want Christians to conduct themselves? The answer, of course, is with a life of holiness.

A life of holiness

Paul gives some fairly pointed advice for living a holy life, which can be summed up under three major headings. Holiness of life is to show itself in

1. Unity among believers (4:1-16);
2. Living a pure life (4:17–5:20);
3. Assuming responsibility in keeping with our Christian status in life (5:21–6:9).

*"There is one body and one Spirit—
just as you were called to one hope
when you were called." (4:4)*

Holiness is to show itself in unity among believers

4 As a prisoner for the Lord, then, I urge you to live a life worthy of the calling you have received. ²Be completely humble and gentle; be patient, bearing with one another in love. ³Make every effort to keep the unity of the Spirit through the bond of peace. ⁴There is one body and one Spirit—just as you were called to one hope when you were called—⁵one Lord, one faith, one baptism; ⁶one God and Father of all, who is over all and through all and in all.

Paul reminds us that he is God's ambassador, commissioned to preach the gospel. He has carried out this task to the extent of being arrested and imprisoned for his efforts. But even being a prisoner doesn't stop him from helping his beloved Ephesians. As their spiritual father and mentor, Paul wants to see a balance between their Christian calling and their daily conduct.

The Ephesians didn't bring themselves to faith. They didn't by themselves find access to the Christian church. No, they were "called" by God's grace. In his love God sent them his Holy Spirit through the gospel Paul preached. The Holy Spirit, who "calls, gathers, and enlightens" people, brought them in. When they were "dead in . . . transgressions and sins" (2:1), the Spirit gave them life—a new life with grand possibilities. Because the Ephesians have this new life in Christ, Paul can expect a proper response from them when he says, "I urge you to live a life worthy of the calling you have received."

What kind of life does Paul—or, rather, God—expect? Paul lists four qualities, divided into two pairs.

First Paul says, "Be completely humble and gentle." The realization of their own unworthiness before God would humble them, and in that spirit of humility they are to be

177

gentle toward others. These two are internal qualities, characteristics that the Ephesians bring to the scene.

The next two qualities involve irritations and aggravations from others. Here Paul urges, "Be patient, bearing with one another in love." The key to having patience and putting up with others is love. Again, the Greek word used here is that one-way love that doesn't look for anything in return. It simply reflects to others the undeserved one-way love we have received from a gracious God (see 4:32; also Colossians 3:12-14, especially verse 13).

Why should the Ephesians put themselves out for irksome and irritating brothers? Paul points out that there is a great deal at stake. He urges, "Make every effort to keep the unity of the Spirit through the bond of peace."

Nothing less than "the unity of the Spirit" is at stake. When Paul speaks of the "unity of the Spirit," we need to be very clear that this is a unity the Holy Spirit has accomplished. It is the unity that exists in the holy Christian church, into which the Holy Spirit has brought all believers in Christ. It is not something dependent on us or something we create by our right actions and conduct. It does not come about because *we* "make every effort to keep the unity." Rather, Paul cautions us not to spoil the *Holy Spirit's* good work by our own actions and lose the unity *he* establishes by disrupting the peace with petty quarrels and inconsiderate actions.

Just how great and precious that unity is becomes apparent when Paul says it is the masterpiece of the triune God. All three persons of the Godhead—Father, Son, and Holy Spirit—were involved in effecting this unity. Paul shows this in a table beginning at verse 4. He constructs three sets of three items each—one set for each person of the Trinity. Interestingly enough, he reverses the order from what we're used to seeing. He places the persons into this sequence: Spirit, Son, Father.

178

In the first set Paul highlights the Spirit's contribution to the church's unity by assembling three items, all introduced by the numerical adjective "one." He says, "There is *one* body and *one* spirit*—just as you were called to *one* hope when you were called." We have noted that the Holy Spirit calls, gathers, and enlightens people. Twice Paul in this verse reminds the Ephesians that they were "called." They were called into one body, the holy Christian church. In that body all people are of the same heart and mind—of "one spirit," if you will—because they all have one and the same hope, namely, eternity with God in heaven.

Regarding the second member of the Trinity, Paul sets up this triad: "*one* Lord, *one* faith, *one* baptism." In Luther's explanation of the Second Article of the Apostles' Creed we confess that Jesus purchased and won us, not with gold or silver, but with his holy precious blood. And he did this so that we might be his own. He owns us. He is our *Lord*, and the only Lord we want or need. Furthermore, all believers by definition believe in him. He is the *object of their faith.* "Salvation is found in no one else, for there is no other name under heaven given to men by which we must be saved" (Acts 4:12). And the way to come to faith in Christ is through the means of grace, through Word and sacraments. In stressing the unity that exists among members of the church Paul calls special attention to *baptism*, very likely because it is the universal sacrament, intended for all age groups.

---

*We have preferred to use the lowercase "spirit." The Greek language was written with either all capital letters or all lowercase letters, so it is impossible to determine from the Greek letters whether Paul intended "Spirit" or "spirit." Since the three items seem to refer not to the Spirit himself but to draw our attention to three things the Holy Spirit has brought about, the lowercase "spirit" seems more appropriate here. The term will then refer to the attitude, the mind-set, in believers.

In his third triad Paul varies the form, giving us three prepositions to highlight our gracious God's activity. There is only one God, our heavenly Father, "who is *over* all and *through* all and *in* all." With his almighty power our heavenly Father looks after all and watches *over* them. With his matchless grace he works *through* his believers to accomplish his saving purpose. In fact, so close is the relationship between God and his believers that Paul can even say God dwells *in* his believers. As bold and daring as that sounds, Paul really is saying nothing other than what Jesus himself promised his followers at the Last Supper: "If anyone loves me, he will obey my teaching. My Father will love him, and we will come to him and make our home with him" (John 14:23).

Paul's point in this whole section is that a marvelous unity binds the Ephesians to one another (in their local congregation, or "visible church") and binds them also to every other believer in the worldwide holy Christian church (the "invisible church"). Therefore, in their daily sanctified lives the Ephesians shouldn't do anything to spoil this great blessing. Rather, they should "make every effort to keep the unity of the Spirit through the bond of peace."

Despite this unity that binds together all believers in Christ, believers always retain their own individuality. They are not reduced to a number in God's book. He knows each believer by name. He treats each one with the utmost love and care.

⁷But to each one of us grace has been given as Christ apportioned it.

God's saving grace is without bounds or limits, but the grace whereby he distributes gifts to men for the upbuilding of the church is "as Christ apportioned it." In other words, different people receive different portions to carry out their God-given opportunities to help build the church. That thought will be developed more fully in verses 11 to 13. First, however, Paul wants to call attention to the Source of those gifts. The Giver is none other than the risen, triumphant, ascended Lord Christ. Paul substantiates that from Scripture.

> [8]This is why it says:
>
> > "When he ascended on high,
> > he led captives in his train
> > and gave gifts to men."
>
> [9](What does "he ascended" mean except that he also descended to the lower, earthly regions? [10]He who descended is the very one who ascended higher than all the heavens, in order to fill the whole universe.)

Paul draws attention to the fact that when Psalm 68:18 speaks of God as "ascended," the psalmist implies that God first "descended to the lower, earthly regions." Bible scholars are somewhat divided on what is meant by "descended." Some see this as Christ's triumphant descent into hell on Easter morning to proclaim his victory over sin, death, and Satan. Christ's descent into hell is certainly a doctrine clearly taught in Scripture (1 Peter 3:19,20), and it is possible that is referred to here.

Paul's emphasis in this section, however, is on Christ's exalted return to heaven, where he now fills "the whole universe." Hence it seems somewhat more likely that the apostle's reference to a "descent" is rather to Christ's state of humiliation—in contrast to his present state of exaltation. Paul would then be speaking of Christ's descending to earth to be our Substitute, living a perfect life, and dying an innocent death for us, so that he could declare, "It is finished" (John 19:30). Finished was his mortal combat with Satan, sin, and death. He captured these great enemies who long had tyrannized us and held our sinful race hostage. He lorded over these defeated foes in triumphal procession at his Ascension. They cannot prevent Christ from implementing his stated plan of having the good news of the gospel carried out to the whole world (Matthew 28:16-20; Mark 16:15).

Risen, ascended, and sitting at the right hand of the Father, Christ now fills the whole universe. He is totally in charge. But, marvel of marvels, he deigns to give us mortals a part in his grand plan to have the church spread out into all the world. To empower his church for this important task he "gave gifts to men." These gifts are the "portions" his grace has determined his representatives need to carry out their various tasks.

Paul proceeds to list some of the gifts Christ has given to serve his cause.

¹¹It was he who gave some to be apostles, some to be prophets, some to be evangelists, and some to be pastors and teachers,

It would be an engaging process to try to find names of people who might fit the categories Paul lists, but his intent seems rather to list offices or positions Christ created for the church.

Bible scholars have tried to determine meaningful distinctions between the five terms listed here. Some general distinctions can be made on the basis of examining the roots of the Greek words used. An "apostle" is someone sent out or commissioned. New Testament usage suggests that a "prophet" was not necessarily a person who foretold the future but one who brought God's message to others, be that a message about the past, present, or future. "Evangelists" are people who share the gospel (from *euangelion*, which we translate "gospel"). An attempt is also made to group the terms. Apostles, prophets, and evangelists are understood to be traveling ministers, whereas pastors and teachers are assumed to serve in one specific location. Perhaps that is true. It is possible that the specific descriptions of the offices Paul lists do not conform exactly to what we have today.

Two things, however, can definitely be asserted about all the positions Paul names: they were part of the public ministry and they were instituted ("given") by Christ. Hence the public ministry is they were divinely instituted. It did not come about through tradition, nor was it merely the church's response to needs that arose. In practice the public ministry may take different forms, but it is a divine institution given to the church by our ascended Lord.

Why did he institute the public ministry?

12to prepare God's people for works of service, so that the body of Christ may be built up 13until we all reach unity in the faith and in the knowledge of the Son of God and become mature, attaining to the whole measure of the fullness of Christ.

God's purpose in establishing the public ministry was "that the body of Christ may be built up." As noted previously, the "body of Christ" is picture language describing the organic unity of all believers in Christ, that is, the church. God wants that unity to be strengthened and realized ever more fully. To that end he established the public ministry positions listed in verse 11.

These public servants are shepherds who feed and protect the flock, as well as search out the lost and straying. But they aren't to be the only ones doing the work, nor do they do it all by themselves. As part of their work, God has also directed them "to prepare God's people for works of service." Or as we might also put it, to prepare God's people for *service-work*.

183

God's people serve their fellow Christians by using God's Word to help them grow in their faith. That Word is "useful for teaching, rebuking, correcting and training in righteousness" (2 Timothy 3:16). Everyone is his brother's keeper—and to do that in the best possible way requires training or preparation for service-work.

What is the goal or outcome of this service-work? Paul describes the ideal toward which we strive when he says, "Until we all reach unity in the faith and in the knowledge of the Son of God and become mature, attaining to the whole measure of the fullness of Christ."

With the pronoun "we" Paul switches to the first person, thereby including himself. To be sure, he is writing to the Ephesians, but what he is saying here applies to himself and to all other Christians as well.

Paul enumerates three components that comprise the goal toward which we all should strive. But they are not three separate things. They all speak of the desired "building up" that is to take place as Christians help one another through faithful use of the Word.

Paul first describes this building up as something occurring "until we all reach unity in the faith and in the knowledge of the Son of God." Knowing Christ and believing in him are the key ingredients to bringing about the growth God looks for in his church.

As faith and knowledge about Christ grow, believers "become mature." That process, however, is never complete here on earth. It has rightly been said that the Christian life is a constant "becoming." Paul himself hadn't yet attained full spiritual maturity—as he frankly admits to the Philippians (3:12-15). For a candid statement of his frustration with his frequent lapses and lack of maturity, read Romans 7, particularly verses 14 to 25. Spiritual maturity is not fully attainable here, but it is what every Christian strives for personally and seeks to help others reach.

Paul's third component in the goal toward which we are striving is that we all "[attain] to the whole measure of the fullness of Christ." We might paraphrase that expression by saying, "Until we reach Christ's full stature." Again, that won't happen this side of heaven.

Speaking the truth in love

Paul not only gives positive advice and encouragement, but he points out that there is a dark side, yes, a real danger, in not growing up spiritually. He sketches that for us in a series of vivid pictures that describe the grave situation from which spiritual maturity spares us.

14Then we will no longer be infants, tossed back and forth by the waves, and blown here and there by every wind of teaching and by the cunning and craftiness of men in their deceitful scheming.

People who don't grow spiritually through diligent use of Word and sacrament remain infants, despite their chronological age. With no doctrinal base, they're helpless because they have nothing firm to hang on to. That's why Paul can liken them to people in a rowboat out on the high seas during a fierce gale. They're swept around "by every wind of teaching."

Or, to change the picture a bit, spiritually immature people are like unsophisticated buyers being "worked" by a slick salesperson. Because they don't know the product, they're taken in "by the cunning and craftiness of men in their deceitful scheming." Without knowing it, immature Christians may not be getting pure doctrine or correct teaching. They may be accepting spiritual snake oil from false teachers. Not a good situation at all!

185

But there is help. Paul gives us the remedy and antidote.

15Instead, speaking the truth in love, we will in all things grow up into him who is the Head, that is, Christ.

Far from accepting false doctrine, spiritually mature Christians will rather go on the offensive against it. They will "[speak] the truth in love."

Let's take a moment to review Paul's line of thought in this chapter. He has stated that the ascended Christ (verse 10) gave gifts to his church in the form of public ministers (verse 11). These public servants of the Word are to prepare God's people for service-work (verse 12), so that they, in turn, can help others. Paul has help from rank-and-file Christians in mind when he refers to people "speaking the truth in love."

It is important that such speakers not only be correct (speak the truth) but also that they speak "in love." They are not to lord it over their weaker brothers. Nor are they viciously to turn on false teachers, but rather speak as lovingly and as winsomely as possible in the hope of winning over the proponent of an incorrect view. Then the unity will be kept, and growth in the church will be effected.

To be sure, it is the Christians who do the speaking, but God grants the results. Paul points that out when he reminds us that all growth and increase in the body, the church, comes from Christ, its Head. He asserts:

16From him the whole body, joined and held together by every supporting ligament, grows and builds itself up in love, as each part does its work.

Paul makes it clear that every Christian has a role in Christ's church. We need to keep that in mind. We're often inclined to think that we're too small or too unimportant to make much of a difference. Paul helps us understand how wrong that kind of thinking is. *"Every* supporting ligament" is important to the body. The whole body grows and builds itself up "as *each* part does its work." Every Christian is an important part of the church, because growth and improvement in the church come "from him," that is, from Christ, and not from us.

The converse, of course, is also true. The church suffers when any Christian wastes his God-given gifts and doesn't do his part. Again, we need only think of the analogy to the human body. Think of what misery and discomfort the whole body feels when one member is sick or fails to function properly.

Holiness is to show itself in living a pure life

In chapters 1 to 3 Paul rehearsed for the Ephesians the great things their Savior and Redeemer God has done for them in giving them spiritual life and bringing them into the Christian church.

In chapters 4 to 6 Paul helps them understand what their response should be to such grace. What is expected of them is, to summarize it in one word, holiness. Paul has already urged them to show such holiness by striving to keep the unity of the Spirit through the bond of peace (4:1-16).

Now he advances to a second area of emphasis: holiness that reflects itself in the purity of their lives and conduct. Very earnestly he warns them:

[17]So I tell you this, and insist on it in the Lord, that you must no longer live as the Gentiles do, in the futility of their thinking. [18]They are darkened in their understanding and separated from the life of God because of the ignorance that is in them due to the hardening of their hearts. [19]Having lost all sensitivity, they have given themselves over to sensuality so as to indulge in every kind of impurity, with a continual lust for more.

187

It is important to realize that the holiness Paul is advocating is not to be done in order to gain favor with God or improve our standing before him. Our redemption and salvation have been completely taken care of by Christ's work. But is it merely optional that the redeemed child of God confirm his life to God's holy will? No! As God's representative, Paul tells the Ephesians, and "[insists] on it in the Lord," that they are no longer to live as the Gentiles do, "in the futility of their thinking."

The problem with the Gentiles was that they had no proper set of values. Their thinking was all messed up. Paul attaches a devastating description to them. He charges them with being *darkened* in their understanding, *separated* from God, *ignorant* because they have *hardened* their hearts.

With such a wrong set of values and with such wrong thinking, it was inevitable that they would become guilty of wrong actions. Paul continues, "Having lost all sensitivity, they have given themselves over to sensuality so as to indulge in every kind of impurity, with a continual lust for more."

Although it is not evident from the NIV translation, in the Greek "*having lost* all sensitivity" is an active form of the verb. It is not that their sensitivity was taken from them; they abandoned it. The next clause also has an active verb: "They have given themselves over to sensuality." The Gentiles did what they wanted to, but, instead of satisfying them, it simply heightened their desire for more. Paul's point is that Gentiles in their pagan lifestyle were hopelessly enmeshed in immoral ways.

The Ephesians, of course, were Gentiles and came from precisely the kind of pagan society Paul describes. But in their case a wonderful change had taken place, a change that did not originate in any way from paganism. Their changed and improved status came from Christ and the body of

Christian doctrine that Paul and other gospel preachers brought to them. Paul invites the Ephesians to reflect on how that change came about.

²⁰You, however, did not come to know Christ that way [via paganism]. **²¹Surely you heard of him and were taught in him in accordance with the truth that is in Jesus. ²²You were taught, with regard to your former way of life, to put off your old self, which is being corrupted by its deceitful desires; ²³to be made new in the attitude of your minds; ²⁴and to put on the new self, created to be like God in true righteousness and holiness.**

We'll catch the point of these five verses if we reduce them to the main line of thought: "You were taught . . . to put off your old self . . . and to put on the new self."

Paganism did nothing to bring the Ephesians to their present fortunate state. That came only when they learned of Christ, when they "were taught . . . in accordance with the truth that is in Jesus." Christ's truth was totally at odds with the values of their "former way of life."

Recall Paul's telling the Ephesians that Gentiles not only give themselves over to sensuality but also enjoy their depravity, continually lusting for more (verse 19). The reason for that lies in the fact that the old Adam, that is, natural, unregenerate man, "is being corrupted by . . . deceitful desires."

The desires are "deceitful" because Satan is behind them, and he makes promises on which he doesn't deliver. Satan has a dozen bogus reasons for the sinner to go ahead and sin: it will be enjoyable; it will be profitable; it's fashionable; everybody's doing it; no one will be hurt by it; etc. All these promote wrong thinking. Hence, they're "deceitful."

There is only one remedy, and that's the Christian solution that was taught to the Ephesians: "to put off your old self, which is being corrupted by its deceitful desires; to be made new in the attitude of your minds."

Duped by Satan, natural man (the "old self") is not able to make the change Paul is promoting here. That change can come only through the law-gospel message that the Ephesians had been taught by Paul and his coworkers. A clear exposition of God's holy law had informed them how far out of line they were in their sinful lives. And the realization of their wickedness had struck fear and terror into their hearts when they realized the just consequences of their sins.

But with such people—terror-stricken sinners—Paul and his coworkers could share the gospel. They could inform the Ephesians, as the Prophet Nathan did King David, "The LORD has taken away your sin" (2 Samuel 12:13), or as John the Baptist did when he directed his hearers to Christ with the words "Look, the Lamb of God, who takes away the sin of the world!" (John 1:29).

Paul now appeals to people of a new attitude of mind, people who are looking in faith to Christ, the Lamb of God. He urges them "to put on the new self, created to be like God in true righteousness and holiness." The "new self" is the converted, regenerated child of God, whose newfound reverence and love for God enables him to want to do what God wants done. Note that this new man has been "created." He is not someone the Christian has brought into being. He has been brought into being by God's almighty, creative power.

And what God has created is intended "to be like God in true righteousness and holiness." This new creation is a return to the image of God in which man and woman were created (Genesis 1:27), but which they lost when they fell into sin. Unfortunately, this restoration will not be complete here on earth, because we Christians all too often succumb to temptation (note Paul's experience, Romans 7), but it is a

start. The new man has a keen desire to live in the true righteousness and holiness that pleases his Redeemer-God.

Paul appeals to this desire to please a gracious and loving
God when in the next section he urges a life of sanctification.
Aware of the many evil situations that engage Christians
every day, Paul chooses some representative examples of the
kind of evil they are to put off and the kind of holiness in living that God would have them put on.

Examples of pure living

**25Therefore each of you must put off falsehood and speak
truthfully to his neighbor, for we are all members of one body.
26"In your anger do not sin": Do not let the sun go down while
you are still angry, 27and do not give the devil a foothold. 28He
who has been stealing must steal no longer, but must work,
doing something useful with his own hands, that he may have
something to share with those in need.**

"Shading the truth a bit" and "adjusting the facts" are common weaknesses among people. They should not, however,
be the Christian's way of doing things. Dishonesty is especially damaging when it occurs among believers, "for we are
all members of one body." To deceive a fellow Christian is
really to harm ourselves, because just as in the human body
all the members work together for the common good, so it is
also in the church. Being dishonest with another Christian is
like shooting ourselves in the foot.

Many things stir Christians to righteous anger. They cannot stand idly by while God's name is taken in vain or his
Holy Word is taught falsely. They rightly become angry
when children are neglected or abused. They feel indigna-
tion when owners are defrauded of their property. The danger, however, is that righteous anger can turn into hatred and
vengeful reprisal. Satan would love to see that! It gives him

191

a "foothold." Quoting Psalm 4:4, Paul urges that anger not be allowed to fester. Rather, if at all possible, the matter causing the anger should be addressed that very day, before it has the opportunity to turn into something sinful (see also Luke 12:58).

Bringing home a few "supplies" from work in a lunch bucket is not a new problem. Paul urges the thief to give up his pilfering ways and put in an honest day's labor. Although it is by no means his main point, it is interesting to see how Paul asserts the dignity of manual labor. In the Greek world such tasks were left largely to women and slaves. For the men, a dignified and meaningful occupation meant being out in public life. Paul doesn't reflect that point of view. The Christian, Paul says, will engage in any kind of honest labor, including "doing something useful with his own hands." Then he won't have to take from others, but he'll have enough for himself and can even "share with those in need."

[29]Do not let any unwholesome talk come out of your mouths, but only what is helpful for building others up according to their needs, that it may benefit those who listen. [30]And do not grieve the Holy Spirit of God, with whom you were sealed for the day of redemption. [31]Get rid of all bitterness, rage and anger, brawling and slander, along with every form of malice.

Sanctified living involves the whole person, including how he handles his tongue. It includes *what* he says as well as *how* he says it. Controlling the tongue is not an easy task. James acknowledges that when he writes, "No man can tame the tongue. It is a restless evil, full of deadly poison" (James 3:8). Natural man can't tame the tongue, but the Holy Spirit can. And he does so in the new man, who is active in the Christian. Paul is appealing to that new man when he urges the Ephesians to "not let any unwholesome talk come out of [their] mouths."

Unwholesome talk grieves the Holy Spirit. He has done his sanctifying work of calling, gathering, and enlightening people. He has made them his own and set his seal of ownership on them by dwelling in them. His goal is to keep them safely in the Christian fold "for the day of redemption," that is, until judgment day. Christians who engage in unwholesome talk jeopardize not only their own faith; they also put the faith of others at risk. Rather than harm others by unwholesome talk, Christians are to speak "only what is helpful for building others up according to their needs."

This reminds us of what Paul shared with his readers earlier in this chapter. The ascended Christ gave his church public servants of the Word who are to prepare God's people for service-work, part of which is strengthening others through the gift of speech. Talking to others is a key part of the process. This does not mean getting up on a soapbox and making ourselves ridiculous or obnoxious. Quiet, ordinary, day-to-day conversation reflecting Christian insights and value-judgments can do much to "benefit those who listen."

Talking often discloses the evil in a person's heart and mind. But whether its damaging presence is shown by talk or by actions, Paul strongly urges the Ephesians, "Get rid of all bitterness, rage and anger, brawling and slander, along with every form of malice."

³²Be kind and compassionate to one another, forgiving each other, just as in Christ God forgave you.

5 Be imitators of God, therefore, as dearly loved children ²and live a life of love, just as Christ loved us and gave himself up for us as a fragrant offering and sacrifice to God.

Instead of being bitter and angry with our neighbor, or using loud and insulting speech, Paul urges God's people to be kind, compassionate, and forgiving. That's not easy! After all, we're talking here about a fellow Christian who has committed real sins against us. She has lied about us and spoiled our reputation; he has defrauded us in a business deal. Her abuse of alcohol has deprived our family of the support it needs. Don't we have some rights? Doesn't he or she deserve some of the anger and bitterness we feel?

Paul tries to help the Ephesians in this important area of sanctification by bringing up a well-known and winsome picture. We've all been intrigued by the sight of a toddler trying to imitate his father—pounding a hammer, throwing a ball, raking leaves. Paul is suggesting something similar when he advocates kindness and compassion, love and forgiveness. He says, "Be imitators of God." Do as your Father has done for you. He urges the Ephesians to be forgiving of one another "just as in Christ God forgave you." He urges them to live a life of love "just as Christ loved us and gave himself up for us as a fragrant offering and sacrifice to God."

What our Father has done—that makes all the difference in the world! His actions not only set a pattern and serve as a model, but they give loveless sinners new hearts and new minds. It is God who creates the new man in Christians, who now have the power and the ability to forgive a repentant brother or sister.

And Christians will do it. They will not merely go through the motions, but forgive sincerely—from their hearts. They can do so because they are now living a life of love, in imitation of their heavenly Father. "We love because he first loved us" (1 John 4:19).

³**But among you there must not be even a hint of sexual immorality, or of any kind of impurity, or of greed, because these are improper for God's holy people. ⁴Nor should there be obscenity, foolish talk or coarse joking, which are out of place, but rather thanksgiving. ⁵For of this you can be sure: No immoral, impure or greedy person—such a man is an idolater—has any inheritance in the kingdom of Christ and of God. ⁶Let no one deceive you with empty words, for because of such things God's wrath comes on those who are disobedient. ⁷Therefore do not be partners with them.**

When Paul directed his readers to what God has done for them and asked that they become imitators of God, he was clearly advocating what is *proper* activity for God's holy people. In this section the apostle returns once more to prohibitions and warnings against what is *improper*. A significant segment of his concern has to do with infractions of the Sixth Commandment.

Paul states that there should not be a hint of sexual immorality or impurity among God's people. They are not only to avoid *doing* evil, but they are to avoid even the *appearance* of doing evil. Paul even goes a step farther. Not only are the Ephesians to avoid immoral activity, they are not to debase God's gift of sexuality by making it the subject of humor and coarse jokes. Note how Paul returns again to the subject of controlling the tongue. The tongue is not to be used for spoiling God's gifts but, rather, to thank and praise him for his goodness.

We usually think of greed as being an inordinate desire for money or material things. Paul, however, makes an interesting observation here when he indicates that, in a manner of speaking, the inordinate desire for sexual gratification could be called "greed" as well. In that case, what should be God's good gift to man has in fact become his god. It's what he lives for and what controls his life. Such a person, in the final analysis, is an idolater and sins against the First Commandment as well as the Sixth. The idolater who seeks his highest joy and greatest satisfaction from a false god cannot expect anything from the true God. He has no "inheritance in the kingdom of Christ and of God."

That assessment of the situation holds true, no matter how much the old Adam in sinful men and women may argue against it. All kinds of defenses are made for promiscuous sex, for living together outside marriage, and for alternate lifestyles. Paul says, "Let no one deceive you with empty words." Those arguments will not hold up before God's final bar of justice. Rather, for such things "God's wrath comes on those who are disobedient." For the Ephesians and for us Paul's message is clear: "Do not be partners with them."

⁸For you were once darkness, but now you are light in the Lord. Live as children of light ⁹(for the fruit of the light consists in all goodness, righteousness and truth) ¹⁰and find out what pleases the Lord. ¹¹Have nothing to do with the fruitless deeds of darkness, but rather expose them. ¹²For it is shameful even to mention what the disobedient do in secret. ¹³But everything exposed by the light becomes visible, ¹⁴for it is light that makes everything visible. This is why it is said:

> **"Wake up, O sleeper,**
> **rise from the dead,**
> **and Christ will shine on you."**

When Paul says, "You were once darkness," he is using a figure of speech called a metaphor. Notice what the figure of speech does for Paul's line of thought. Formerly the Ephesians were spiritually in the dark regarding God's will for them. But when Paul says, "[They] were once darkness," he is taking it a step farther. Not only were they misled and under the influence of wicked paganism, they themselves were a bad influence. They were the darkness that misled others to practice and even enjoy gross immorality and wickedness.

Understanding Paul's metaphor about darkness makes the parallel metaphor regarding light all the more striking. The Ephesians were not only enlightened by knowing Christ; they themselves have become light. Not only were they influenced by his gospel, but they themselves are now the influence that builds up their brothers in the church and wins new converts.

Remember Christ's declaration to his disciples: "You are the salt of the earth. . . . You are the light of the world" (Matthew 5:13,14). He didn't say, "You really should be the salt of the earth" or "Strive to become the light of the world." He said, "You *are* the light of the world." Because God's people *are* light, Paul can urge, "Live as children of light (for the fruit of the light consists in all goodness, righteousness and truth) and find out what pleases the Lord." This sentence has two slight complications in it. First, NIV translators have put part of this verse into parentheses. This is helpful because it indicates that Paul is telling us in advance what he means by a life that "pleases the Lord" (verse 10).

In another respect, however, the NIV translators have not been quite so helpful. Their rendering "*find out* what pleases the Lord" could be misleading. This could give the impression that there is considerable unclarity as to what pleases the Lord, and it is our task to discover it. Actually, the Greek verb in this phrase might better be translated "approve" or "put your stamp of approval on." The sense of the sentence would then be: Live as children of light and put your stamp of approval on what pleases God. What pleases God is the fruit that light produces, namely, goodness, righteousness and truth.

By virtue of their being light, God's people are both a positive influence toward those things that please God and also a

197

strong deterrent against those things that do not please God, namely, the fruitless "deeds of darkness."

Just like light, darkness also bears "fruit," all those wicked and worthless things Paul has been warning against. Because those things bring no lasting good or blessing, Paul labels them as "fruitless" or useless.

He therefore bids the Ephesians to have nothing to do with such deeds. They are not merely to avoid them, though; they are also to take positive and decisive steps against them. As light discloses what is hidden under the cover of darkness, so they are to expose the sinful deeds of darkness for what they really are, dangerous and negative influences that are to be rooted out.

Children of light don't relish this task. It is "shameful" even to speak about the evils that need to be combatted and exposed by the light of God's truth. But we have a wholesome purpose for doing this. Our hope is that sinners may see the error of their ways, repent, and turn in faith to the forgiveness that Christ has earned for even the vilest and darkest of misdeeds.

That wholesome and saving intent is reflected in Paul's quotation. The source of this quotation is unknown, but it may be from one of the very early Christian hymns. Whatever the source, it's a winsome invitation, both for the careless Christian who is sleeping in apathy and for the crass pagan who is still dead in transgressions and sins. Both need the same remedy: Christ's light shining into their hearts, which wakes the apathetic Christian and raises to life those who are spiritually dead in unbelief.

Paul is reaching the close of a major section of his letter, a section in which he has stressed the need for personal purity in the lives of his readers. Paul has not appealed to purity so that we *will become* acceptable to God, but so that our lives exhibit purity appropriate for people who by faith in Christ *have been* accepted by God. Out of love and appreciation for what Christ has done for us, we will want to conform our lives to God's holy will.

So Paul wraps up this section with something of a summary:

> **[15]Be very careful, then, how you live—not as unwise but as wise, [16]making the most of every opportunity, because the days are evil. [17]Therefore do not be foolish, but understand what the Lord's will is.**

"[Understanding] what the Lord's will is" and living according to it—that is wisdom. To do otherwise would be "unwise" and "foolish," a lapse back into darkness, a return to the pagan cesspool from which the Ephesians have just recently been rescued.

To be sure, "the days are evil," but the Ephesians also have opportunities. These come in two forms. One is the opportunity for their own spiritual growth, which Paul will be enlarging on in verse 19. Another is the opportunity to witness to their many heathen neighbors who still need to hear the good news of a Savior. Paul urges the Ephesians to pursue both avenues zealously.

> **[18]Do not get drunk on wine, which leads to debauchery. Instead, be filled with the Spirit. [19]Speak to one another with psalms, hymns and spiritual songs. Sing and make music in your heart to the Lord, [20]always giving thanks to God the Father for everything, in the name of our Lord Jesus Christ.**

Intemperance was a besetting sin among the ancients, just as it is today. There can be no doubt that in this verse Paul is sounding a bona fide warning against the misuse of alcohol. But because of where this admonition is placed in Paul's list, it seems also to serve as a backdrop for another encouragement, perhaps an even more important one.

By using the word "instead," Paul joins two somewhat parallel lines of thought. He says: Don't misuse alcoholic spirits to give yourself a bogus kind of lift, a temporary sort of high that leads to all kinds of bad things. "Instead" be filled with the real Spirit to guide you in wholesome activity that brings lasting benefit to you and others.

Paul then proceeds to enumerate the activities that result from being filled with the Spirit. In the Greek those activities are expressed with participles. Literally Paul writes: Be filled with the Spirit, *speaking* to one another with psalms, *singing and making* music, and always *giving thanks*. (Note that there is another activity in the series, "*submitting* to one another out of reverence for Christ" [verse 21], but that will be treated in the next section.)

Filled with the Spirit, the Ephesians are to "speak to one another with psalms, hymns and spiritual songs." Paul suggests that the use of biblical psalms be supplemented with hymns and spiritual songs. There is probably no great difference between hymns and songs. Both are expressions of Spirit-taught truth set in artistic form, which the Ephesians themselves or other Christians had developed.

Although Paul does not specify where or how this activity of "speaking to one another" is to occur, he does seem to imply that a public worship life with liturgical forms was being developed and used (see 1 Corinthians 14:26). We should also note that Paul once more stresses the importance of the proper use of the tongue. At least three times in this letter Paul has touched directly on that subject (4:25,29; 5:4), each time in the context of using speech to help build one another up to keep the unity of the Spirit through the bond of peace (here again note 1 Corinthians 14:26).

Speaking to one another (including public worship life) has its counterpart in private activity. A joyous response wells up in the hearts of redeemed children of God whenever they think of the great blessings they have received. Although not a syllable is spoken or a single note sounded, in their upbeat outlook and cheerful devotion to duty Christians "sing and make music in [their hearts] to the Lord."

Somewhat along the same lines, Paul urges that the Christian life be marked by "always giving thanks to God the Father for everything, in the name of our Lord Jesus Christ." Let's not forget that Paul himself acknowledged that "the days are evil." All kinds of things can discourage, irritate, and disappoint Christians, harried as they are by the devil and the world and hampered by their own sinful flesh. But filled with the Spirit, they know that "in all things God works for the good of those who love him, who have been called according to his purpose" (Romans 8:28). Daily they can rise and confidently say, "This is the day the LORD has made; let us rejoice and be glad in it" (Psalm 118:24).

Holiness is to show itself in assuming responsibilities

Paul has at some length described the life and conduct that our Savior God rightly expects of people who appreciate what his grace has done for them. Theirs will be a life of holiness that in ever greater degree conforms with God's holy, unchangeable will.

So far, Paul has pointed to two general areas of sanctification in the Christian life: preserving the unity that exists among believers, since all are members of the same body, and living a morally pure life.

Paul now advances to a third area: living a life that accepts the responsibilities God has placed on us in our particular station of life. In the next 22 verses (5:21–6:9) the apostle will be dealing with three pairs of relationships: husbands and wives, parents and children, employers and employees. As a broad, overarching directive for this area he says,

²¹Submit to one another out of reverence for Christ.

Recall that Paul encouraged the Ephesians to "be filled with the Spirit . . . speak to one another with psalms . . . sing and make music in your heart . . . giving thanks to God." The series now continues, "Submit to one another out of reverence for Christ."

What is being asked in this Table of Duties, as it is often called, is something that only the Christian, moved by the Holy Spirit, can do. Only the Christian knows what is the proper thing to do, and only the Christian is truly motivated to do it. "Submit," Paul says, "out of reverence for Christ." In all six of the following categories of responsibility, reverence for Christ must be our motivating force. Otherwise we will find the responsibilities irksome and restrictive.

Wives

²²Wives, submit to your husbands as to the Lord. ²³For the husband is the head of the wife as Christ is the head of the church, his body, of which he is the Savior. ²⁴Now as the church submits to Christ, so also wives should submit to their husbands in everything.

To understand these two verses one needs to arrive at answers to two questions: What does it mean to "submit" and why should a wife submit to her husband?

In English it is hard to reflect the more neutral tone of the Greek verb we translate as "submit." All our English verbs tend to convey some negative connotations. The root meaning of the Greek verb means simply "to rank people or things *in order* under some specific pattern." It does not imply inferiority or lesser value, as our English verbs too easily suggest. To "be subordinate" might come closest to reflecting the Greek.

All comparisons limp, but a situation from the sports world can perhaps bring us a step closer to grasping the meaning of "submit." Take the case of a pitcher and catcher on a baseball team. Both are on the same side and have the same objective; both want to make their contribution to winning the game. But the things they do are quite different!

Usually it's the catcher who decides what pitch should be thrown. The pitcher "submits" to that decision. That doesn't mean he can't ever "shake off" a pitch or that there might not be an occasional conference at the mound, but in general, the catcher calls the pitches.

Does that mean the catcher is better than the pitcher? Is the pitcher inferior because he submits to the catcher's selection of pitches? Not at all! That's simply the way things work best. They both recognize that each can't be doing his own thing if they want to win the ball game. Somebody has to decide whether a fast ball or a change-up is more likely to strike Casey out. It's a matter of assigned roles, a designated order of things. That's the essence of team play.

Marriage is certainly a team project. The God of order who instituted it has designated the manner in which it will be most harmonious and function with the greatest blessing. In his wisdom he has delegated headship, or the leadership role, to the husband. "Submission" on the wife's part is simply acknowledging that God-given role relationship.

"But why should a wife submit to her husband?" some grumble. By nature all of us are inclined to inject our notions of equality and our ideas of "fairness" and conclude God is imposing an unfair arrangement on women. But Paul is not talking to natural man or unregenerate people here. He is confident that his readers are filled with the Spirit and are people who understand when he urges them to submit "out of reverence for Christ." He is confident the feeling of unfairness will flee when he brings Christ into the picture.

Christ is the head of the church, and as the church submits to Christ, so also wives should submit to their husbands. In the next section addressed to husbands, Paul will say much more about Christ's gentle and loving treatment of the church. For the moment it's sufficient for him to draw the parallel and assume that everyone will reach the proper conclusion: The church's submitting to Christ is not a demeaning thing but something that brings great blessing. Such is the case also in a marriage where the wife accepts the headship of her husband.

Unfortunately, even at their best, husbands can't begin to hold a candle to Christ's love for the church. But the pattern, the model of what a Christian husband should be, is clearly indicated. Paul now proceeds to enlarge on what Christ has done for the church and urge it as a pattern and guide for husbands to follow.

Husbands

25Husbands, love your wives, just as Christ loved the church and gave himself up for her 26to make her holy, cleansing her by the washing with water through the word, 27and to present her to himself as a radiant church, without stain or wrinkle or any other blemish, but holy and blameless.

As it is the wife's duty to recognize the leadership role of her husband, so it is the husband's duty to love her. It is important to recognize that we are here again dealing with that beautiful and highly significant Greek word for love, *agape*. Greek has a number of words for "love." One designated mutual love between friends; another, physical attraction. Then there was *agape*, the unselfish, one-way love we previously discussed—God's totally unselfish love for us (2:4,5; 4:2). God's *agape* moved him to give us great and precious blessings, not because we could return and requite his love but simply out of his boundless goodness and mercy. His unselfish love moved him to do all that for us.

Now Paul says, "Husbands, love your wives, just as Christ loved the church and gave himself up for her." Christ showed the ultimate in unselfish love by what he was willing to do for the church. He gave up his life to win her for himself. However, he not only purchased her for himself at the price of his life blood, but he raised her to a most enviable position. He "cleansed her by the washing with water through the word." Through the means of grace, Word and sacrament, he cleansed her of her many transgressions, forgave her sin, quieted her conscience, gave her peace with God, and assured her of security in his protecting hand.

But what he has done for her on earth is only a small foretaste of what he still has in mind for her. On judgment day he will present her as a bride—not to someone else, but to himself. Then she will be a "radiant church," without any stain from the outside or wrinkle developed on the inside. She will not have any blemish but will be "holy and blameless."

With Christ's unselfish love for the church serving as a backdrop, Paul now says, "In this same way, husbands ought to love their wives." Christlike leadership leaves absolutely no room for a husband to be a dictator or tyrant. As he looks to Christ's example of headship over the church, he will find no basis to be selfish or domineering. Nor will he be unconcerned about his wife's needs or unappreciative of what she brings to the marriage team.

It will be evident that if a husband is to fulfill his leadership role as Paul outlines it, he has his work cut out for him! Fortunately, Christ's love is not only the pattern and example, but it also provides the motivation to do what God asks and the strength to put that resolve into practice. To be sure, every husband—sinner that he is—will be imperfect. But Christ's love will compel him daily to strive for the ideal illustrated by our Savior's love for the church. With God's help husbands can begin to approximate that.

Christ's unselfish love is certainly the compelling argument here. But it's interesting to see Paul add a second argument, one on a somewhat lower level. It's almost as if Paul were saying: If the example of Christ's unselfish love isn't enough for you, then you might consider another angle—a selfish one.

[28]In this same way, husbands ought to love their wives as their own bodies. He who loves his wife loves himself. [29]After all, no one ever hated his own body, but he feeds and cares for it, just as Christ does the church—[30]for we are members of his body. [31]"For this reason a man will leave his father and mother and be united to his wife, and the two will become one flesh."

Paul quotes Genesis 2:24 to make the point that when two people marry, they don't remain separate entities any longer. It wouldn't be logical for them each to remain at home with their parents. The only thing that makes sense is for both of them to cut the ties with their parents so as to set up their own new household. The two have essentially become one.

Since the two are in essence one, "husbands ought to love their wives as their own bodies." It's just the natural thing to do. Everybody looks after his own needs. He eats and sleeps, dresses and grooms himself. Shouldn't a husband just naturally show the same kind of devoted care and concern for his other "self," or as we might say, for the rest of himself?

³²This is a profound mystery—but I am talking about Christ and the church. ³³However, each one of you also must love his wife as he loves himself, and the wife must respect her husband.

We have previously noted that when Paul uses the term "mystery" he is not talking about something dark or mysterious, something impossible to understand. Rather, he's referring to something that needs explanation, something we couldn't ever have figured out by ourselves. When it's explained, it becomes clear and comprehensible.

The "profound mystery" that Paul is speaking of is not primarily that marriage unites husband and wife into one. No, his thoughts have swung back to Christ and the church. The real mystery is the one-way love of Christ. He redeemed weak and worthless sinners and gathered them together into a church to be his holy bride. He is her head; she is his body. So closely are the two joined into one.

In quiet awe Paul reflects on the mystery of Christ and the church—and on the fact that there can be in the human experience something that reflects this divine unity and even approximates it. That something is a Christian marriage in which the husband loves "his wife as he loves himself" and his wife respects him as her husband.

Although that ideal is not fully attainable in our sinful world, it is a goal all married people should diligently strive for.

Children

6 **Children, obey your parents in the Lord, for this is right. ²"Honor your father and mother"—which is the first com-**

mandment with a promise—³"that it may go well with you and that you may enjoy long life on the earth."

From a section outlining the duties of wives and husbands, Paul logically proceeds to a section on children and parents. Although it is not a particularly weighty point, there is a bit of disagreement among Bible scholars on the placement of the phrase "in the Lord." The NIV translation puts it with the parents, giving it the meaning, "Children, obey the parents whom the Lord has given you." That is certainly possible.

Others link "in the Lord" with the children. Paul would then be urging children who are "in the Lord" to obey their parents. That pairing is what underlies a translation such as, "Children, obey your parents because you are Christians" (God's Word). In view of the fact that this section of the Table of Duties concerns itself with the sanctified lives of children, the latter interpretation addressing them as Christians is perhaps to be preferred.

Either way, Paul is addressing the "new man" (or should we say, "new child"?) in young people and urging them to obey their parents. The reason given is simply "for this is right." It is right because the Lord says so. He has given children life, a home, and parents.

But children are not merely to "obey" their parents, perhaps unwillingly and grudgingly. More is asked of Christian children. They are to "honor" their parents. Thus a proper attitude is required, one that involves both heart and mind.

That the Lord is serious about having the Fourth Commandment obeyed is evident from the fact that he attaches a promise to it. Paul's quotation of the commandment and the promise is taken from Deuteronomy 5:16. While the original promise recorded there speaks to Israel and refers to the Promised Land, the general truth holds for all times. That

208

doesn't mean every child who obeys his or her parents will necessarily live to be a hundred. But the converse is true: disobedience to parents has bad consequences. Since the family is the basis of society and thus also of the nation, woe to the people and the land that disregard this fundamental relationship between parents and children.

Fathers

⁴Fathers, do not exasperate your children; instead, bring them up in the training and instruction of the Lord.

When Paul in this section addresses "fathers," he is speaking to them in their role as the head of the household. Mothers, of course, are by no means excluded or assumed to be less active in bringing up the children. Recall that in the previous verse the apostle called on children to obey their "parents"—not just their fathers. We may therefore fairly understand this section of the Table of Duties to be addressed to both parents. Paul's directives to parents take two forms, a negative followed by a positive.

Paul begins, "Do not exasperate your children." Indeed, parents are in charge, but that doesn't mean that they're always fully informed or that they might not at times have used better judgment. Temperamental outbursts and undue harshness on the part of parents can do major harm to tender souls.

Instead of exasperating and frustrating children, parents are to "bring them up in the training and instruction of the Lord." The Greek word translated "training" implies discipline and correction. It would be naive of parents to expect that such training will always be welcome. Recall the Scriptures' comments regarding the acceptance of "chastisement" (Hebrews 12:7-13, particularly verse 11). But in the long run, treatment that is fair and consistent will be helpful, particularly as that is combined with the "instruction of the Lord."

Parents always need to remember that children have an old Adam who needs to be curbed with God's law. But through Baptism and basic instruction from the Word, children also have a new man who cheerfully responds to God's will as it is conveyed to them through God's representatives.

Slaves

5Slaves, obey your earthly masters with respect and fear, and with sincerity of heart, just as you would obey Christ. 6Obey them not only to win their favor when their eye is on you, but like slaves of Christ, doing the will of God from your heart. 7Serve wholeheartedly, as if you were serving the Lord, not men, 8because you know that the Lord will reward everyone for whatever good he does, whether he is slave or free.

Slaves require a major section in Paul's Table of Duties—second only to husbands. That may be because numerically slaves comprised a significant portion of the Ephesian congregation. Certainly in the Graeco-Roman world, permeated as it was with slavery, slaves were an important sociological and economic factor.

It's important to note that Paul does not make it his or the church's platform to abolish slavery. That does not mean Paul put his stamp of approval on it. In Philemon, a letter that may have accompanied our letter to the Ephesians, Paul also addressed the slavery question. There, you may recall, Paul put in a good word for the runaway slave Onesimus, who was returning to his master. Paul not only strongly urged kind treatment for Onesimus but also hinted that his owner, Philemon, might consider releasing him (Philemon 21). Abolishing slavery, however, is not part of Paul's agenda. Far from it. Paul rather urges Christian slaves to be good slaves.

However, a couple factors make slavery more tolerable. First, Paul notes that slaves are serving "earthly masters." Slavery is a temporary situation, only for this world. Furthermore, it's not an indication of a slave's personal value, worth, or status before God. It makes no difference to God whether a person is "slave or free" (verse 8; see also Galatians 3:28). The unity in the church that has been able to bring together Jew and Gentile also equalizes slave and free.

That doesn't mean slavery will always be easy or comfortable. In urging the Ephesian slaves to obey their masters, Paul acknowledges that they may well be doing it "with respect and fear" (literally, with fear and trembling), so it's safe to say some anxiety may be involved. Hence Paul views slavery as a cross, but one to be borne with Christian fortitude and ready acceptance.

In urging a God-pleasing course of action for the trying situation in which slaves find themselves, Paul sounds one negative and encourages with three positives. Initially he cautions them against obeying their masters "only to win their favor when their eye is on [them]." That would be totally self-serving and unacceptable. Rather, they are to let their new man respond and obey their masters "just as [they] would obey Christ."

That total obedience is expected becomes clear from the threefold encouragement to serve their masters *heartily*. Paul tells them to serve "with sincerity of *heart*," "doing the will of God from [their] *heart*," so that they "serve *wholeheartedly*."

How are they to bring themselves to do that? Paul answers, "Because you know that the Lord will reward everyone for whatever good he does, whether he is slave or free."

It is absolutely essential to keep in mind that Paul is writing these words to *Christian* slaves. These words are not directed to unregenerate people, suggesting that they can improve their status before God by good service to masters or that they can put themselves into a position where God owes them a reward. No, Paul is talking about their conscientious service as a fruit of faith, done as if they were "serving the Lord, not men."

Paul's way of expressing that truth is nothing other than what our Savior himself said when he described judgment day as a division between the sheep and the goats. The basis for that division will be the presence or absence of saving faith, as demonstrated by the presence of good deeds or the lack of them. In effect Paul is saying, Everything will be properly sorted out on judgment day. That is an encouragement to slaves, just as it serves as a warning to masters who may be inclined to mistreat their slaves.

Masters

⁹And masters, treat your slaves in the same way. Do not threaten them, since you know that he who is both their Master and yours is in heaven, and there is no favoritism with him.

When Paul here writes to "masters," he is addressing Ephesian slave owners who are Christian. His intent is not to indict them for having slaves but rather to encourage Christian conduct toward slaves—the more so if their slaves are fellow Christians (think again of Philemon).

Paul urges masters to conduct themselves "in the same way." That parallel carries us back into the section addressed to slaves. As slaves were to lead thoroughly Christian lives as they fulfilled their duties, so masters too were to be guided by Christian principles.

Such Christian principles rule out the threats by masters that no doubt were often a contributing factor to the "fear" we heard about on the part of slaves. Masters are not to terrorize their slaves. To make his point Paul utilizes a play on words involving the term "lord" or "master." He says in effect: Be careful in your conduct. Even though you are a master over your slaves, don't forget that there is in heaven someone who is your Master as well as theirs—and he doesn't play favorites.

Even the Christian retains an old Adam who needs to be restrained by God's law. Such restraint is what this short but sharp section is intended to provide for Ephesian slave owners. The real improvement, however, has to come from a heart that appreciates what the Master in heaven has done in sending his Son. Where that Master controls the slaves' master, there will be no mistreatment of slaves. In this way Christianity rendered tolerable what was basically a worldly institution all too open to abuse.

It will be evident that much of what Paul says in these last two sections transfers directly to the employer-employee relationships in today's workplace.

Courage to contend against evil, wearing God's armor

Paul often alerts us that he is coming to the close of a letter by introducing his concluding section with the adverb "finally." We have that signal at verse 10.

Recall that in the entire second half of his letter Paul has been speaking of the blessed effect that God's saving grace has on the life of his believers. The new life of the children of God will show itself in a life of holiness. Their holiness is committed to keeping the Spirit-worked bond of unity and to leading a life of personal purity. And as we have most recently seen, their holiness shows itself in being willing to shoulder the responsibilities God gives them, whether that be as husband or wife, child or parent, employer or employee.

213

Paul closes his letter by pointing out one final effect of God's saving grace, namely, making God's people willing to contend *for* the faith and *against* evil. For that they need some special equipment—equipment God provides.

The armor of God

¹⁰Finally, be strong in the Lord and in his mighty power. ¹¹Put on the full armor of God so that you can take your stand against the devil's schemes. ¹²For our struggle is not against flesh and blood, but against the rulers, against the authorities, against the powers of this dark world and against the spiritual forces of evil in the heavenly realms.

As a final, general word to his readers Paul says, "Be strong." The Christian life will always be a struggle. Attacks on the faith will take the form of temptations and moral lapses. There will be temptations to yield on points of doctrine. There will be temptations to formalize religion and reduce it to an external thing, a mere shell. There will be temptations of lovelessness toward fellow believers and hatred toward those who are not believers. The list could go on, but the point is clear: we need to be strong against temptations.

That, however, is not something children of God can do by themselves. They need help—God's help. Hence Paul says, "Put on the full armor of God so that you can take your stand against the devil's schemes."

We're often inclined to think that our problems and opposition come from perverse people. Evil people, however, are really only agents and instruments. They're part of Satan's scheme against believers. Paul says it plainly: "Our struggle is not against flesh and blood, but against the rulers, against the authorities, against the powers of this dark world and against the spiritual forces of evil in heavenly realms." We are battling spiritual forces bent on doing us harm. That

214

"Put on the full armor of God so that you can
take your stand against the devil's schemes." (6:11)

shouldn't surprise us. Scripture tells us of a group of angels who fell (Revelation 12:7-9) and are now under the leadership of Satan, who "prowls around like a roaring lion looking for someone to devour" (1 Peter 5:8).

It is a battle of cosmic proportions ("in the heavenly realms"), but that needn't dismay us, for the help on our side is cosmic also. Recall that the apostle opened this letter with the glorious sentence "Praise be to the God and Father of our Lord Jesus Christ, who has blessed us *in the heavenly realms* with every spiritual blessing in Christ" (1:3). The help is there; we need only avail ourselves of it.

13Therefore put on the full armor of God, so that when the day of evil comes, you may be able to stand your ground, and after you have done everything, to stand. 14Stand firm then, with the belt of truth buckled around your waist, with the breastplate of righteousness in place, 15and with your feet fitted with the readiness that comes from the gospel of peace. 16In addition to all this, take up the shield of faith, with which you can extinguish all the flaming arrows of the evil one. 17Take the helmet of salvation and the sword of the Spirit, which is the word of God.

Paul here brings the cosmic battle down to the individual encounters the Christian is caught up in "when the day of evil comes," that is, when he is assailed by sharp temptation or opposition. It is then that he will need a good defense system.

The military items Paul enumerates were the standard equipment of an infantryman in the Roman army. He mentions five pieces of defensive armor and one offensive weapon. The five defensive pieces combined make up the "full armor" that Paul uses as his picture of the spiritual protection God provides for the believer.

In its literal, military sense the "belt . . . around your waist" is the section of armor strapped on to protect the soldier's midsection and thighs, whereas the "breastplate" covered his upper body. He had his "feet fitted" with appropriate shoes or boots and wore a "helmet" to protect his head. He used a round shield to ward off sword and spear thrusts or to deflect flying missiles in the form of arrows or thrown javelins.

Paul attaches spiritual significance to the various pieces of military hardware. He does not seem to intend that the "belt" should stand for "truth" and nothing else, or that the "breastplate" can represent only "righteousness." Rather, Paul is drawing together the various aspects of Christ's redemptive work that the Christian is to rally to when he comes under attack. Hence we need not try to find distinguishing features among "truth," "righteousness," and "salvation." Nor need we search for some difference between "faith" and the "readiness" which the gospel brings. The power is God's, and it's all there for us. Paul's point is, When attacked, look to Christ's work as your defense.

However, the Christian doesn't just have to hunker down and ride out the storm. He has one weapon of offense—and he needs no other! He has the "sword of the Spirit, which is the word of God." Armed with this, he not only can defend himself but go on the offensive as well, for that Word is "living and active. Sharper than any double-edged sword, it penetrates even to dividing soul and spirit, joints and marrow" (Hebrews 4:12).

Using God's Word, the Christian can rout any of the "powers of this dark world" or the "spiritual forces of evil in the heavenly realms." It only remains for him to be faithful in his use of the Word and regularly to turn to his almighty Lord in prayer.

217

Prayer

18And pray in the Spirit on all occasions with all kinds of prayers and requests. With this in mind, be alert and always keep on praying for all the saints.

19Pray also for me, that whenever I open my mouth, words may be given me so that I will fearlessly make known the mystery of the gospel, 20for which I am an ambassador in chains. Pray that I may declare it fearlessly, as I should.

All kinds of incorrect notions abound as to what prayer is and what can be expected of it. The apostle gives the Ephesians important instruction on both points.

He opens by telling them to "pray in the Spirit." What he is advocating is not some dramatic or showy charismatic praying. Rather, he is indicating that only through Christ can anyone properly approach the triune God. An essential feature of prayer is that it comes from a heart filled with faith (James 1:6,7; Hebrews 11:6). And faith, of course, is something that only the Holy Spirit can work. Spirit-worked faith takes God at his word, trusts his promises, and confidently approaches him as a dear heavenly Father. All this meshes perfectly with what Paul wrote earlier: "Through him [Christ] we both [Jew and Gentile] have access to the Father by one Spirit" (2:18).

What may a Christian pray for? People generally feel it is fitting to come to God with "important" things and in times of emergency. But other than that, they don't want to bother him. They reason: Surely, he can't be interested in the little problems I have. Besides, I should be able to take care of those myself. Note, however, what Paul says: "Pray in the Spirit on *all occasions* with *all kinds* of prayers and requests."

Few directives are given more often or more pointedly in Scripture than the invitation and encouragement to pray. The Lord promises: "Call upon me in the day of trouble; I will deliver you, and you will honor me" (Psalm 50:15). Our Savior solemnly assured his disciples and us, "Ask and it will be given to you; seek and you will find; knock and the door will be opened to you" (Luke 11:9). Peter encourages his readers, "Cast all your anxiety on him because he cares for you (1 Peter 5:7). Elsewhere Paul says, "Pray continually; give thanks in all circumstances, for this is God's will for you in Christ Jesus" (1 Thessalonians 5:17,18).

In the area of spiritual matters, such as forgiveness of sins, the gift of a good conscience, conversion of unbelievers, or unity in the church, we know that it is God's gracious will to give us those things. In temporal matters, however, we will always add the condition "if it is your will." Such prayers are answered—in God's good time and in his way.

Because the Ephesians have the precious privilege of prayer, as do all Christians, Paul exhorts them, "With this in mind, be alert and always keep on praying for all the saints." The "saints" are fellow believers with the Ephesians, ones who, like them, have been made holy by faith in Christ's merits. Paul asks the Ephesians to pray for all of them and requests a special prayer for one particular saint—himself: "Pray also for me, that whenever I open my mouth, words may be given me so that I will fearlessly make known the mystery of the gospel, for which I am an ambassador in chains. Pray that I may declare it fearlessly, as I should."

Recall that the apostle Paul is writing this letter from Rome, where he is under house arrest and awaiting trial for preaching the gospel. Much rests on the outcome of his case—not only for himself personally (see Philippians 1:21-24) but especially for the Christian church. Paul is, in a real sense, "an ambassador in chains." He is representing Christ and his gospel. With this in mind he urges the Ephesians, "Pray that I may declare it fearlessly, as I should."

FINAL GREETINGS
(EPHESIANS 6:21-24)

²¹Tychicus, the dear brother and faithful servant in the Lord, will tell you everything, so that you also may know how I am and what I am doing. ²²I am sending him to you for this very purpose, that you may know how we are, and that he may encourage you.

Paul was not a robot or an automaton. He was very warm and personable and very interested and concerned about people. He realizes people are anxious about him as he awaits trial. He tries to alleviate that concern by sending Tychicus "for this very purpose, that you may know how we are, and that he may encourage you."

We wish we knew more about Tychicus, who earns the high praise of being "the dear brother and faithful servant in the Lord." He is mentioned in four other New Testament passages. Three of them are only passing references (Acts 20:4; 2 Timothy 4:12; Titus 3:12). The fourth, Colossians 4:7-9, deserves a little closer look. There the apostle writes: "Tychicus will tell you all the news about me. He is a dear brother, a faithful minister and fellow servant in the Lord. I am sending him to you for the express purpose that you may know about our circumstances and that he may encourage your hearts. He is coming with Onesimus, our faithful and dear brother, who is one of you. They will tell you everything that is happening here." The first thing that strikes us here is the marked similarity to the Ephesian passage. That, of course, is true of many passages in Colossians. The specific point of overlap here is that Tychicus is to explain Paul's circumstances to both the Ephesians and the Colossians.

Note also another interesting fact. In Colossians, Onesimus is said to be accompanying Tychicus. Recall our earlier discussion of Onesimus, the runaway slave turned Christian whom Paul was sending back to his Christian master, Philemon. Paul says of Onesimus that he is "one of you [Colossians]."

Thus the following scenario emerges: The main "transaction" at this point is Paul's sending Onesimus back to his master, Philemon, who lives in Colosse. Tychicus is carrying a cover letter (our New Testament Philemon) to smooth the delicate matter of a repentant Onesimus being received back into the household of Philemon. This matter may also have repercussions in the local congregation in Colosse, so Paul sends the congregation a letter too, our New Testament Colossians. Incidentally, note the large section on slaves in that letter's Table of Duties (Colossians 3:22-25). Tychicus is carrying both letters to the city of Colosse. To get there, he will have to travel right through Ephesus. Paul seems to be taking the opportunity to write a parallel letter to his beloved Ephesians, among whom he had worked for three years (Acts 20:31). Thus Tychicus, in fact, seems to be carrying three letters, Ephesians, Colossians, and Philemon, as he escorts Onesimus back home to Colosse.

²³Peace to the brothers, and love with faith from God the Father and the Lord Jesus Christ. ²⁴Grace to all who love our Lord Jesus Christ with an undying love.

To the section on taking up the whole armor of God Paul added a reminder regarding the importance of prayer. "Be alert," he told the Ephesians, "and always keep on praying for all the saints." Paul practiced what he preached. The parting thought in his letter is in reality an intercessory prayer. He prays for the Ephesians and all believers in Christ whom the Spirit has united into that great unity, the holy Christian church. Paul's prayer for them all is that they may receive "peace . . . and love with faith."

Those are not earned or deserved rewards. They are gifts from a loving God, who in Christ is moved to give "immeasurably more than all we ask or imagine" (3:20). Included among those immeasurable and unimaginable gifts is nothing less than heaven itself. Such love from our Redeemer-God calls forth but one response, that we love him who loved us first. Paul has in mind all who respond in that way when he closes his prayer and his letter with the petition "Grace to all who love our Lord Jesus Christ with an undying love."